NOTE

1. All recipes serve two unless otherwise stated.

2. All spoon measurements are level.

3. All eggs are sizes 1 and 2 (large) unless otherwise stated, although smaller sizes can be used without disrupting the recipe too seriously.

4. Metric and imperial measurements have been calculated separately. Use one set of measurements only as they are not exact equivalents.

5. Cooking times may vary slightly depending on the individual oven. Dishes should be placed in the centre of the oven unless otherwise specified.

6. All flour is plain and all sugar is granulated (unless otherwise stated).

7. Always preheat the oven or grill to the specified temperature.

8. Spoon measures can be bought in both imperial and metric sizes to give accurate measurement of small quantities.

Cooking for Two

Rosemary Wadey

TREASURE PRESS

Contents

First published in 1978 by
Sundial Publications Ltd

This edition published in 1985 by
Treasure Press
59 Grosvenor Street
London W1

© 1978 Hennerwood Publications Ltd

ISBN 1 85051 043 1

Printed in Hong Kong

Introduction

At one time or another, most people will want to prepare a meal for two – be it to entertain a new friend, or for an anniversary, or every day if you are just two. But most recipes serve four, or even six, and can be difficult to halve.

The recipes in this book are designed for just those situations, ranging from simple and quick dishes to more sophisticated fare for special occasions, and all of them serve two.

Quickly cooked dishes are ideal for two people, but they are not always economical – expensive cuts of meat cook the most quickly.

Careful planning is necessary so fuel is not wasted when cooking in small quantities. You will find lots of ideas in the Poultry and Meat chapter for both meals in moments and more elaborate dishes. For example, if you want to serve baked potatoes for dinner, cook a casserole or roast a joint of meat in the oven at the same time – or bake a cake.

Planning is necessary, too, when shopping. If you want to roast a joint of meat or a bird, do not buy such a large one that you will have a lot left over. Remember this rule when buying perishable foods – eggs, butter, cheese, etc. which, bought in bulk, may not be an economy if there

are just two of you to eat them.

Finally, consider your time in the kitchen. It may be possible to double a recipe, serve half, and store the remainder in the refrigerator for a few days, or freezer for months. Soups, pâtés, quiches, casseroles and some desserts in this book are particularly suitable for this. In this way you can put together an appetizing meal in next to no time.

SOUPS

It is easy to open a can of soup, heat it up quickly and eat it, with a chunk of bread and cheese for a quick snack. But that cannot give the satisfaction – and flavour – of eating your own soup made from scratch. It does take longer, but some homemade soups can be on the table in only 15 minutes. Nowadays with the excellent varieties of stock cubes available, you can even cut out the job of making stock. (For those who like the flavour a homemade stock imparts to soup, a recipe follows.)

Although the recipes in this book will serve two (except where stated otherwise), when making soup it is often a good idea to double or even treble the quantities to make a good batch at one time. Once made and cooled, the surplus soup will keep for 2 to 3 days in the refrigerator and much longer if you have a freezer.

A garnish makes a soup appetizing and attractive. Chopped fresh parsley or chives, grated cheese, carrot or hard-boiled egg, fried or toasted croûtons, or a swirl of cream will add that special finish. The suggestions given in the recipes here may be altered according to your taste. For example, for a change, try crisply fried and crumbled bacon rinds, grated orange or lemon rind, coarsely grated apple, chopped salted peanuts, or fried breadcrumbs mixed with herbs.

Basic household stock

Metric

500 g bones from a roast joint or bird, or raw bones and lean meat trimmings (for a light stock, use only veal bones)
1–2 large onions, peeled and chopped
1–2 carrots, peeled and sliced
1 leek, sliced
1 celery stalk, sliced or ½ parsnip, peeled and chopped
1 bouquet garni
Salt
Pepper

Imperial

1 lb bones from a roast joint or bird, or raw bones and lean meat trimmings (for a light stock, use only veal bones)
1–2 large onions, peeled and chopped
1–2 carrots, peeled and sliced
1 leek, sliced
1 celery stalk, sliced or ½ parsnip, peeled and chopped
1 bouquet garni
Salt
Pepper

Cooking Time: About 3 hours

Put the bones and vegetables in a large saucepan and cover with cold water. Add the bouquet garni and salt and pepper to taste. Bring to the boil, skimming any scum from the surface. Cover and simmer for about 3 hours.
Strain the stock and allow to cool. Store in the refrigerator for up to 2 days. Before using, remove any fat which has formed on the surface.

Variation:
For a dark stock, first brown the bones in a preheated hot oven (230°C, 425°F, Gas Mark 7). Fry the vegetables in 1 × 15 ml spoon (1 tablespoon) dripping until well browned. Proceed as above.

Vichyssoise

Metric	Imperial
1 large leek	1 large leek
25 g butter or margarine	1 oz butter or margarine
1 small onion, peeled and thinly sliced	1 small onion, peeled and thinly sliced
225 g potatoes, peeled and diced	8 oz potatoes, peeled and diced
450 ml chicken stock	¾ pint chicken stock
Salt	Salt
Freshly ground black pepper	Freshly ground black pepper
1 mace blade	1 mace blade
1 egg yolk	1 egg yolk
6 × 15 ml spoons single cream	6 tablespoons single cream
Chopped fresh chives to garnish	Chopped fresh chives to garnish

Cooking Time: About 40 minutes

Remove most of the green part of the leek. Slice the white part thinly. Melt the butter or margarine in a saucepan and add the leek and onion. Fry very gently until soft but not coloured. Add the potatoes, stock, salt and pepper to taste and mace and bring to the boil. Cover and simmer gently for about 30 minutes or until tender.

Discard the mace, cool slightly, then sieve or liquidize the soup and return to a clean saucepan. Whisk the egg yolk and cream together, then whisk gradually into the soup. Reheat gently to just below boiling point and adjust the seasoning. Allow to cool, then chill thoroughly. Serve sprinkled with chives.

Note: This soup can also be served hot.

Creamed cucumber soup

Metric	Imperial
½ small cucumber, diced	½ small cucumber, diced
450 ml chicken stock	¾ pint chicken stock
1 small onion, peeled and chopped	1 small onion, peeled and chopped
15 g butter or margarine	½ oz butter or margarine
15 g plain flour	½ oz plain flour
1 × 5 ml spoon lemon juice	1 teaspoon lemon juice
Salt	Salt
Freshly ground black pepper	Freshly ground black pepper
3–4 × 15 ml spoons single cream	3–4 tablespoons single cream
Coarsely grated cucumber to garnish	Coarsely grated cucumber to garnish

Cooking Time: About 25 minutes

Put the diced cucumber, stock and onion into a saucepan. Bring to the boil, cover and simmer for 20 minutes or until tender. Cool slightly, then liquidize or sieve until smooth. Melt the butter or margarine in another saucepan. Stir in the flour and cook for 1 minute. Gradually stir in the cucumber purée and bring to the boil. Add the lemon juice, then season well with salt and pepper and simmer for 4 to 5 minutes. Add the cream and reheat gently without boiling. Serve sprinkled with grated cucumber.

Note: This soup can also be served chilled, in which case, add the cream just before serving.

Vichyssoise; Creamed cucumber soup

Creamed curry soup

Metric

25 g butter or margarine
1 large onion, peeled and
chopped
1 large carrot, peeled and
chopped
1 garlic clove, crushed
1–1.5 × 5 ml spoons curry
powder
1 × 15 ml spoon plain
flour
450 ml chicken stock
2 × 5 ml spoons lemon
juice
Salt
Freshly ground black
pepper
Dash of Tabasco sauce
1 bay leaf
150 ml single cream

To garnish:
Few unpeeled prawns or
fried bread croûtons
Chopped fresh parsley

Imperial

1 oz butter or margarine
1 large onion, peeled and
chopped
1 large carrot, peeled and
chopped
1 garlic clove, crushed
1–1½ teaspoons curry
powder
1 tablespoon plain flour
¾ pint chicken stock
2 teaspoons lemon juice
Salt
Freshly ground black
pepper
Dash of Tabasco sauce
1 bay leaf
¼ pint single cream

To garnish:
Few unpeeled prawns or
fried bread croûtons
Chopped fresh parsley

Cooking Time: 25–30 minutes

Melt the butter or margarine in a saucepan. Add the onion, carrot and garlic and fry gently until soft but not coloured. Stir in the curry powder and flour and cook for 1 minute. Gradually stir in the stock and bring to the boil. Add the lemon juice, salt and pepper to taste, Tabasco and bay leaf. Cover and simmer gently for about 20 minutes or until the vegetables are soft.

Discard the bay leaf and cool the soup slightly, then sieve or liquidize. Leave until cold and adjust seasoning. Stir in the cream and chill thoroughly. Serve garnished with unpeeled prawns or croûtons and then sprinkle with parsley.

Note: To serve this soup hot, reheat after sieving or liquidizing, add cream and bring to just below boiling point.

Quick gazpacho

Quick gazpacho

Metric

2 × 15 ml spoons lemon juice
2 × 5 ml spoons wine vinegar
1 × 2.5 ml spoon Worcestershire sauce
600 ml canned tomato juice
1–2 garlic cloves, crushed
3 large tomatoes, skinned and finely chopped
5 cm piece cucumber, grated or chopped
1–2 × 15 ml spoons finely grated onion
½ green pepper, cored, seeded and finely chopped
Salt
Freshly ground black pepper
Few ice cubes

To garnish:
Chopped fresh herbs
Chopped cucumber, pepper and tomato

Imperial

2 tablespoons lemon juice
2 teaspoons wine vinegar
½ teaspoon Worcestershire sauce
1 pint canned tomato juice
1–2 garlic cloves, crushed
3 large tomatoes, skinned and finely chopped
2 inch piece cucumber, grated or chopped
1–2 tablespoons finely grated onion
½ green pepper, cored, seeded and finely chopped
Salt
Freshly ground black pepper
Few ice cubes

To garnish:
Chopped fresh herbs
Chopped cucumber, pepper and tomato

Put the lemon juice, wine vinegar and Worcestershire sauce into a bowl and add the tomato juice and garlic. Mix well. Stir in the tomatoes, cucumber, onion and green pepper and mix well. If a smooth soup is preferred, liquidize at this stage. Season to taste. Cover the bowl tightly and chill thoroughly.

To serve, pour into a bowl over 2 to 3 ice cubes and sprinkle with chopped herbs. Serve the chopped vegetables separately to sprinkle over the soup.

Serves 4

Note: This soup keeps well in the refrigerator in a covered bowl for 2 to 3 days. It does not freeze.

Creamed curry soup

Spinach soup

Metric	Imperial
25 g butter or margarine	1 oz butter or margarine
1 small onion, peeled and chopped	1 small onion, peeled and chopped
1 × 225 g packet frozen chopped spinach	1 × 8 oz packet frozen chopped spinach
100 g potato, peeled and diced	4 oz potato, peeled and diced
450 ml chicken stock	¾ pint chicken stock
Salt	Salt
Freshly ground black pepper	Freshly ground black pepper
Little grated nutmeg	Little grated nutmeg
1 × 5 ml spoon lemon juice	1 teaspoon lemon juice
150 ml single cream	¼ pint single cream
Croûtons to garnish	Croûtons to garnish

Cooking Time: 25–30 minutes

Melt the butter or margarine in a saucepan and add the onion. Fry gently until soft. Add the spinach and heat through gently until thawed. Stir in the potato, stock, salt and pepper to taste, nutmeg and lemon juice. Bring to the boil, cover and simmer gently for about 20 minutes or until the potato is breaking up. If a smooth soup is preferred, sieve or liquidize it. Return to the pan, taste and adjust the seasoning and stir in the cream. Reheat gently. Serve with fried or oven-baked croûtons.

German potato soup

Metric	Imperial
4 streaky bacon rashers, rinds removed, chopped	4 streaky bacon rashers, rinds removed, chopped
1 onion, peeled and thinly sliced	1 onion, peeled and thinly sliced
225 g potatoes, peeled and diced	8 oz potatoes, peeled and diced
600 ml beef stock	1 pint beef stock
1 bay leaf	1 bay leaf
Salt	Salt
Freshly ground black pepper	Freshly ground black pepper
Good pinch of ground mace or grated nutmeg	Good pinch of ground mace or grated nutmeg
3–4 frankfurters, sliced	3–4 frankfurters, sliced
1 × 15 ml spoon chopped fresh parsley	1 tablespoon chopped fresh parsley

Cooking Time: About 35 minutes

Fry the bacon gently in a saucepan until the fat begins to run. Add the onion and continue cooking until it begins to brown lightly. Stir in the potatoes, stock, bay leaf, salt and pepper to taste and mace or nutmeg. Bring to the boil, cover and simmer gently for about 25 minutes or until the potato has broken down. Add the frankfurters, taste and adjust the seasoning and simmer for a further 5 minutes. Remove the bay leaf. Stir in most of the parsley and serve sprinkled with the remainder.

Chilli bean soup

Metric	Imperial
1 × 15 ml spoon oil	1 tablespoon oil
1 medium onion, peeled and finely chopped	1 medium onion, peeled and finely chopped
100 g finely minced beef	4 oz finely minced beef
2 × 5 ml spoons plain flour	2 teaspoons plain flour
1 × 2.5–5 ml spoon chilli powder	½–1 teaspoon chilli powder
300 ml beef stock	½ pint beef stock
1 × 5 ml spoon tomato purée	1 teaspoon tomato purée
Salt	Salt
Freshly ground black pepper	Freshly ground black pepper
1 × 275 g can red kidney beans, well drained	1 × 10oz can red kidney beans, well drained
Chopped fresh parsley to garnish	Chopped fresh parsley to garnish

Cooking Time: About 40 minutes

Heat the oil in a saucepan. Add the onion and fry until soft. Add the beef and cook very gently for 5 to 8 minutes, stirring frequently. Stir in the flour and chilli powder and cook for 1 minute, then gradually stir in the stock and bring to the boil. Add the tomato purée and season well with salt and pepper. Cover and simmer gently for 15 minutes, stirring occasionally. Add the beans and continue cooking for a further 8 to 10 minutes. Add a little more stock if the soup is too thick and adjust seasoning. Serve sprinkled liberally with parsley.

Note: To make this soup into a satisfying supper dish increase the mince to 225 g (8 oz) and serve with boiled rice, noodles or French bread and butter.

German potato soup; Chilli bean soup; Spinach soup

STARTERS

Only two for supper – is it worth making a starter? Yes, because an interesting starter need not take long to prepare, but it will certainly whet the appetite and make you look forward to the next course with enthusiasm and appreciation, not just hunger.

A starter, whether hot or cold, should be light and served in small quantities. Fresh vegetables and salads, and fruits such as melon and grapefruit can be quickly prepared to give a refreshing starter.

The recipes here may be doubled to make snacks or light meals, and the salads may also be served as accompaniments to main courses.

French dressing

Metric	Imperial
150 ml oil	¼ pint oil
3 × 15 ml spoons vinegar	3 tablespoons vinegar
Salt	Salt
Freshly ground black pepper	Freshly ground black pepper
1 garlic clove, crushed	1 garlic clove, crushed
1 × 2.5 ml spoon made mustard	½ teaspoon made mustard
1 × 2.5 ml spoon French mustard	½ teaspoon French mustard
1 × 15 ml spoon lemon juice	1 tablespoon lemon juice
1 × 2.5 ml spoon sugar	½ teaspoon sugar
Dash of Worcestershire sauce	Dash of Worcestershire sauce

Put all the ingedients into a screw-topped jar and shake until well blended. Taste and adjust the seasonings and shake well again before use. The dressing can be further flavoured with freshly chopped herbs, extra garlic, tomato purée, grated orange or lemon rind, etc.
Note: the oil used can be olive, corn or vegetable; and the vinegar either wine, cider, distilled, malt, tarragon or other flavours, as desired.
Makes about 175 ml (6 fl oz).

Victorian cocktail

Minted grape and melon cocktail

Minted grape and melon cocktail

Metric

1 ripe Ogen melon
Few fresh mint leaves
100–175 g black grapes,
halved and seeded

Imperial

1 ripe Ogen melon
Few fresh mint leaves
4–6 oz black grapes,
halved and seeded

Cut the melon in half and remove the seeds. Crush a few mint leaves and put into the melon hollow, then spoon in the grapes. Chill for about 1 hour before serving, garnished with a sprig of mint.

Victorian cocktail

Metric

1 large grapefruit
1 large ripe avocado,
halved and stoned
3 × 15 ml spoons French
dressing
Fresh mint or parsley
sprigs to garnish

Imperial

1 large grapefruit
1 large ripe avocado,
halved and stoned
3 tablespoons French
dressing
Fresh mint or parsley
sprigs to garnish

Cut away all the skin and pith from the grapefruit and remove the segments free of membrane. Cut large segments in half. Put the avocado halves in two dishes, cut sides up. Rub the cut surfaces of the avocado with a little of the dressing to prevent discoloration. Put 1 × 15 ml spoon (1 tablespoon) dressing into each avocado half. Dip the grapefruit into the remaining dressing, then arrange in the avocado hollows. Garnish with mint or parsley sprigs and serve.

Clockwise: Dressed artichokes with Hollandaise sauce; Salami and fennel salad; Mushrooms à la grecque; Apple cocktails

Apple cocktails

Metric

1 green eating apple,
cored and chopped
2 × 5 ml spoons lemon
juice
2 × 15 ml spoons French
dressing
1 large head of chicory,
thinly sliced
1 carrot, peeled and cut
into julienne strips
1 × 15 ml spoon chopped
fresh parsley
½ × 50 g can anchovy
fillets, drained
Fresh parsley sprigs to
garnish

Imperial

1 green eating apple,
cored and chopped
2 teaspoons lemon juice
2 tablespoons French
dressing
1 large head of chicory,
thinly sliced
1 carrot, peeled and cut
into julienne strips
1 tablespoon chopped
fresh parsley
½ × 2 oz can anchovy
fillets, drained
Fresh parsley sprigs to
garnish

Sprinkle the apple with the lemon juice. Add the dressing, then mix in the chicory, carrot and parsley. Cut the anchovies in half lengthways then into 2.5cm (1 inch) pieces. Add to the salad, toss lightly and spoon onto two small plates. Garnish with parsley sprigs and serve.

Mushrooms à la grecque

Metric	Imperial
2 × 15 ml spoons oil	2 tablespoons oil
1 medium onion, peeled and finely chopped	1 medium onion, peeled and finely chopped
1 carrot, peeled and diced	1 carrot, peeled and diced
1 garlic clove, crushed	1 garlic clove, crushed
1 bay leaf	1 bay leaf
4 × 15 ml spoons white wine	4 tablespoons white wine
Salt	Salt
Freshly ground black pepper	Freshly ground black pepper
225 g tiny button mushrooms	8 oz tiny button mushrooms
To garnish:	To garnish:
1–2 tomatoes, skinned and sliced	1–2 tomatoes, skinned and sliced
Chopped fresh parsley	Chopped fresh parsley

Cooking Time: 15–20 minutes

Heat the oil in a saucepan and add the onion, carrot and garlic. Fry gently until soft but not coloured. Add the bay leaf, wine and salt and pepper to taste and bring to the boil. Simmer for 1 minute. Cut any large mushrooms in half, then add them all to the pan. Cover and cook gently for 4 to 5 minutes, shaking the pan frequently.

Discard the bay leaf and adjust the seasoning. Allow to cool, then chill thoroughly. Serve in small dishes garnished with tomato slices and sprinkled with chopped parsley.

Note: Two skinned and chopped tomatoes may be added to the cooling mushrooms. This may also be served as a side salad.

Salami and fennel salad

Metric	Imperial
½ bulb Florence fennel, trimmed and chopped	½ bulb Florence fennel, trimmed and chopped
1 × 15 ml spoon finely chopped onion	1 tablespoon finely chopped onion
1 hard-boiled egg, chopped	1 hard-boiled egg, chopped
6–8 black olives	6–8 black olives
50 g salami, thinly sliced	2 oz salami, thinly sliced
3 × 15 ml spoons French dressing	3 tablespoons French dressing
Few lettuce leaves	Few lettuce leaves
Watercress sprigs to garnish	Watercress sprigs to garnish

Put the fennel in a bowl with the onion, egg and olives. Reserve two slices of salami for the garnish and chop the remainder. Add the chopped salami to the salad with the dressing and toss lightly.

Arrange a bed of lettuce on two plates. Pile the salad in the centres. Garnish with rolls of salami and watercress.

Dressed artichokes

Metric	Imperial
2 globe artichokes	2 globe artichokes
Squeeze of lemon juice	Squeeze of lemon juice
Hollandaise sauce:	Hollandaise sauce:
2 × 15 ml spoons wine vinegar	2 tablespoons wine vinegar
1 × 15 ml spoon water	1 tablespoon water
2 egg yolks	2 egg yolks
75 g butter, softened	3 oz butter, softened
Salt	Salt
Freshly ground black pepper	Freshly ground black pepper

Cooking Time: 20–40 minutes

Cut off the artichoke stems close to the base of the leaves. Remove the outside layer of leaves and any which are dry. Wash well and drain. Cook in boiling salted water with the lemon juice for 20 to 40 minutes (depending on size) or until the leaves pull out easily.

Meanwhile make the Hollandaise sauce. Boil the vinegar and water together until reduced by just over half. Beat the egg yolks and vinegar mixture together and cook gently in a heatproof bowl over hot water until thickened, stirring continuously. Beat in the butter a little at a time and adjust the seasonings. Keep warm.

Drain the artichokes upside down, then serve hot with the Hollandaise sauce. To eat, pull off the leaves one at a time, dip in the sauce and chew the fleshy part off. Remove the choke when it is reached and eat the 'bottom' or heart with a knife and fork.

Variation:
Serve the artichokes with melted butter, to which a squeeze of lemon juice has been added, instead of the Hollandaise.

Mushrooms in port

Metric	Imperial
65 g butter	2½ oz butter
½ onion, peeled and finely chopped	½ onion, peeled and finely chopped
175 g tiny button mushrooms	6 oz tiny button mushrooms
2 × 15 ml spoons port or sherry	2 tablespoons port or sherry
Salt	Salt
Freshly ground black pepper	Freshly ground black pepper
1–2 × 15 ml spoons double cream	1–2 tablespoons double cream
2 slices of bread	2 slices of bread
Chopped fresh parsley to garnish	Chopped fresh parsley to garnish

Cooking Time: 12–15 minutes

Melt 25 g (1 oz) of the butter in a frying pan. Add the onion and fry gently until soft. Add the mushrooms and continue cooking for 2 to 3 minutes. Stir in the port or sherry and salt and pepper to taste and simmer for 3 minutes. Add the cream, reheat gently and adjust the seasoning. Serve hot on pieces of bread fried in the remaining butter. Sprinkle with parsley.
Note: This dish can also be served as a vegetable without the fried bread.

Hot cheese and mushroom soufflés

Metric	Imperial
40 g butter or margarine	1½ oz butter or margarine
1 small onion, peeled and finely chopped	1 small onion, peeled and finely chopped
50 g mushrooms, chopped	2 oz mushrooms, chopped
Salt	Salt
Freshly ground black pepper	Freshly ground black pepper
15 g plain flour	½ oz plain flour
6 × 15 ml spoons milk	6 tablespoons milk
1 × 2.5 ml spoon made mustard	½ teaspoon made mustard
40 g mature Cheddar cheese, grated, or 2 slices of processed cheese, chopped	1½ oz mature Cheddar cheese, grated, or 2 slices of processed cheese, chopped
1 large egg, separated	1 large egg, separated

Cooking Time: About 30 minutes
Oven: 200°C, 400°F, Gas Mark 6

Melt 25 g (1 oz) of the butter or margarine in a frying pan and fry the onion until soft. Add the mushrooms and continue cooking for 2 minutes. Season well with salt and pepper and spoon into two greased large ramekin dishes or a 600 ml (1 pint) soufflé dish. Melt the remaining butter in a saucepan. Stir in the flour and cook for 1 minute. Gradually stir in the milk and bring to the boil. Simmer for 1 minute. Season well, then stir in the mustard and cheese until melted. Remove from the heat and beat in the egg yolk. Beat the egg white until stiff and fold quickly and evenly through the sauce. Spoon over the mushroom mixture and bake in a preheated moderately hot oven for 20 to 25 minutes or until well risen and golden brown. Serve immediately.

Prawns in whisky

Metric	Imperial
25 g butter	1 oz butter
1 small onion, peeled and finely chopped	1 small onion, peeled and finely chopped
100 g peeled prawns	4 oz peeled prawns
2 tomatoes, skinned and chopped	2 tomatoes, skinned and chopped
2 × 15 ml spoons whisky	2 tablespoons whisky
2 × 5 ml spoons lemon juice	2 teaspoons lemon juice
Salt	Salt
Freshly ground black pepper	Freshly ground black pepper
2 pieces of hot toast or a little boiled rice	2 pieces of hot toast or a little boiled rice
Chopped fresh parsley	Chopped fresh parsley
2 unpeeled prawns	2 unpeeled prawns

Cooking Time: 10–15 minutes

Melt the butter in a frying pan. Add the onion and cook very gently until soft but not coloured. Stir in the prawns and tomatoes and cook gently for 2 to 3 minutes, stirring frequently. Add the whisky, lemon juice and salt and pepper to taste and bring to the boil. Simmer for 2 to 3 minutes. Adjust the seasoning and spoon quickly onto pieces of hot toast or rice. Sprinkle with parsley and garnish with an unpeeled prawn.
Note: Sherry or white wine may be used in place of whisky.

Smoked mackerel pâté; Sardine paté; Cod brandade; Creamy chicken liver pâté

Smoked mackerel pâté

Metric

*100 g smoked mackerel
fillet (1 small fillet)
25 g butter
1 × 15 ml spoon finely
chopped onion
1 garlic clove, crushed
(optional)
1 hard-boiled egg, grated
Salt
Freshly ground black
pepper
3–4 × 15 ml spoons soured
cream*

*To garnish:
Tomato slices
Cucumber slices*

Imperial

*4 oz smoked mackerel
fillet (1 small fillet)
1 oz butter
1 tablespoon finely
chopped onion
1 garlic clove, crushed
(optional)
1 hard-boiled egg, grated
Salt
Freshly ground black
pepper
3–4 tablespoons soured
cream*

*To garnish:
Tomato slices
Cucumber slices*

Remove the skin and bones from the mackerel and mash thoroughly. Melt the butter in a saucepan and fry the onion and garlic if using, until soft. Add to the mackerel with the grated egg, salt and pepper to taste and cream and beat well. Put into a small dish, fork up the top and chill until required. Garnish with tomato and cucumber slices. Serve with hot toast or crusty bread.

Sardine pâté

Metric	Imperial
1 × 125 g can sardines drained	1 × 4 oz can sardines, drained
75 g cream cheese, softened	3 oz cream cheese, softened
Pinch of finely grated lemon rind	Pinch of finely grated lemon rind
1 × 15 ml spoon lemon juice	1 tablespoon lemon juice
1 garlic clove, crushed	1 garlic clove, crushed
Salt	Salt
Freshly ground black pepper	Freshly ground black pepper
About 25g butter, melted	About 1 oz butter, melted

To garnish:
Stuffed olives, sliced
Fresh parsley sprigs

Mash the sardines thoroughly, then beat in the cream cheese until smooth. Add the lemon rind and juice, garlic and salt and pepper to taste and beat in well. Divide between two cocotte dishes. Level the tops and cover each with melted butter. Chill until the butter has set. Garnish with sliced olives and a parsley sprig and serve with hot toast fingers or crispbread.

Cod brandade

Metric	Imperial
175 g cod fillet	6 oz cod fillet
Milk	Milk
4 × 5 ml spoons lemon juice	4 teaspoons lemon juice
Salt	Salt
Freshly ground black pepper	Freshly ground black pepper
25 g slice of crustless white bread	1 oz slice of crustless white bread
2 × 15 ml spoons olive oil	2 tablespoons olive oil
1 garlic clove, crushed	1 garlic clove, crushed

To garnish:
Capers
Pickled gherkins

Cooking Time: About 10 minutes

Poach the fish in the minimum of milk with 1 × 15 ml spoon (1 tablespoon) of the lemon juice and salt and pepper until tender. Cool in the cooking liquor. Drain the fish, discard the skin and bones and flake finely. Soak the bread in 2 × 15 ml spoons (2 tablespoons) milk, then squeeze as dry as possible. Mash the bread thoroughly, then beat in the flaked fish until smooth. Gradually beat in the oil, garlic, remaining lemon juice and salt and pepper to taste. Cover and chill thoroughly. Serve garnished with capers and gherkins, with hot toast and butter.

Creamy chicken liver pâté

Metric	Imperial
25 g butter	1 oz butter
1 × 15 ml spoon finely chopped onion	1 tablespoon finely chopped onion
1 garlic clove, crushed	1 garlic clove, crushed
175 g chicken livers, washed and drained	6 oz chicken livers, washed and drained
1 × 15 ml spoon brandy (optional)	1 tablespoon brandy (optional)
Salt	Salt
Freshly ground black pepper	Freshly ground black pepper
2 × 15 ml spoons double cream	2 tablespoons double cream

To garnish:
Lemon twists
Fresh parsley sprigs

Melt the butter in a frying pan. Add the onion and garlic and fry until soft. Add the chicken livers, cover the pan and cook gently for 5 minutes, stirring frequently to prevent sticking. Add the brandy, if using, and cook for a further 5 minutes. Remove from the heat and stir in plenty of salt and pepper and the cream. Sieve, liquidize or thoroughly mash the pâté. Put into two individual dishes. Chill until set, then serve garnished with lemon twists and parsley sprigs.

EGGS AND CHEESE

Eggs and cheese form the basis of many quick-to-prepare meals and snacks, so they are ideal ingredients to have on hand when cooking for two. Scrambled eggs or an omelette are obvious choices, but it takes very little extra time to prepare a more substantial and appetizing main dish from eggs and cheese. Try Mornay eggs or Ranch-style eggs (a mixture of peppers, tomato and onion with baked eggs).

Some of the dishes here can also be prepared in advance and then popped into the oven when required. These include Celery and ham au gratin and Macaroni topkapi. Eggs and cheese can even make up dishes for a special occasion – Orchard cottage soufflé, made with onions, tomatoes and sweetcorn, is both quick and impressive.

Mornay eggs

Metric	Imperial
50 g butter or margarine	2 oz butter or margarine
1 × 15 ml spoon finely chopped onion	1 tablespoon finely chopped onion
50 g mushrooms, chopped	2 oz mushrooms, chopped
Salt	Salt
Freshly ground black pepper	Freshly ground black pepper
Pinch of ground mace	Pinch of ground mace
4 hot hard-boiled eggs	4 hot hard-boiled eggs
25 g plain flour	1 oz plain flour
300 ml milk	½ pint milk
75 g Cheddar cheese, grated	3 oz Cheddar cheese, grated
Few cooked peas to garnish	Few cooked peas to garnish

Cooking Time: About 10 minutes

Melt 25 g (1 oz) of the butter or margarine in a saucepan. Add the onion and mushrooms and fry until soft. Drain off any liquid, then season well with salt, pepper and mace. Halve the eggs lengthways. Remove the yolks and mash well, then stir into the mushroom mixture. Use to stuff the egg whites and sandwich them back together. Place in a flameproof dish.

Melt the remaining butter in a saucepan. Stir in the flour and cook for 1 minute. Gradually stir in the milk and bring to the boil. Simmer for 1 minute. Season well and stir in 50 g (2 oz) of the cheese until melted. Pour over the eggs. Sprinkle with the remaining cheese and brown under a preheated moderate grill. Spoon peas at each end of the dish and serve.

Mornay eggs

Cheese and asparagus pudding

Metric

300 ml milk
50 g fresh white
breadcrumbs
100 g asparagus, cooked
and cut into 1 cm pieces
100 g mature Cheddar
cheese, grated
Salt
Freshly ground black
pepper
Pinch of garlic powder
1 × 5 ml spoon made
mustard
2 large eggs, separated

To garnish:
Cooked bacon rolls
Cooked asparagus tips

Imperial

½ pint milk
2 oz fresh white
breadcrumbs
4 oz asparagus, cooked
and cut into ½ inch pieces
4 oz mature Cheddar
cheese, grated
Salt
Freshly ground black
pepper
Pinch of garlic powder
1 teaspoon made mustard
2 large eggs, separated

To garnish:
Cooked bacon rolls
Cooked asparagus tips

Cooking Time: About 30 minutes
Oven: 200°C, 400°F, Gas Mark 6

Heat the milk to just below boiling point, then remove from the heat. Stir in the breadcrumbs and leave to stand for 20 minutes. Stir the asparagus into the bread mixture with the cheese, salt and pepper to taste, garlic powder, mustard and egg yolks. Beat the egg whites until stiff and fold evenly through the mixture. Spoon quickly into a greased 750–900 ml (1¼–1½ pint) capacity ovenproof dish. Bake in a preheated moderately hot oven for 25 to 30 minutes or until well risen and golden brown. Serve immediately, garnished with bacon rolls and asparagus.

Cheese and asparagus pudding

Macaroni topkapi

Metric	Imperial
75–100 g macaroni	3–4 oz macaroni
40 g butter or margarine	1½ oz butter or margarine
1 onion, peeled and sliced	1 onion, peeled and sliced
50 g mushrooms, sliced	2 oz mushrooms, sliced
25 g plain flour	1 oz plain flour
300 ml milk	½ pint milk
Salt	Salt
Freshly ground black pepper	Freshly ground black pepper
1 × 2.5 ml spoon dried mixed herbs	½ teaspoon dried mixed herbs
75 g matured Cheddar cheese, grated	3 oz matured Cheddar cheese, grated
2 hard-boiled eggs, sliced	2 hard-boiled eggs, sliced
1 tomato, sliced	1 tomato, sliced

Cooking Time: About 40 minutes
Oven: 200°C, 400°F, Gas Mark 6

Cook the macaroni in plenty of boiling salted water until just tender. Drain well. Melt the butter or margarine in a saucepan and fry the onion until soft. Add the mushrooms and continue cooking for 2 minutes, then stir in the flour. Cook for 1 minute. Gradually stir in the milk. Bring to the boil and simmer for 2 minutes. Season very well. Stir in the herbs and 50 g (2 oz) of the cheese then mix in the cooked macaroni.

Pour half the mixture into a greased ovenproof dish. Cover with most of the sliced eggs, then the remaining macaroni mixture. Sprinkle with the remaining cheese and bake in a preheated moderately hot oven for 25 to 30 minutes or until the top is lightly browned. Garnish with the remaining slices of egg and the tomato and serve hot.

Baked Spanish omelette

Metric	Imperial
2 tomatoes, skinned and chopped	2 tomatoes, skinned and chopped
1 large potato, peeled, cooked and chopped	1 large potato, peeled, cooked and chopped
½ green pepper, cored, seeded, chopped and blanched	½ green pepper, cored, seeded, chopped and blanched
50 g Cheddar cheese, grated	2 oz Cheddar cheese, grated
1 × 5 ml spoon chopped fresh or dried chives	1 teaspoon chopped fresh or dried chives
4 eggs, beaten	4 eggs, beaten
Salt	Salt
Freshly ground black pepper	Freshly ground black pepper
15 g butter or margarine	½ oz butter or margarine

Cooking Time: 10–15 minutes
Oven: 220°C, 425°F, Gas Mark 7

Mix together the tomatoes, potato, green pepper, cheese and chives in a bowl. Add the eggs and salt and pepper to taste and mix well. Use the butter or margarine to grease a shallow ovenproof dish and pour in the egg mixture. Bake in a preheated hot oven until the omelette is just set. Do not overcook. Serve at once.

Note: Other ingredients such as chopped cooked ham or chicken, peas, beans, carrots, etc. may be added or substituted for the above.

Orchard Cottage soufflé

Metric	Imperial
50 g butter or margarine	2 oz butter or margarine
1 onion, peeled and sliced	1 onion, peeled and sliced
2 tomatoes, skinned and sliced	2 tomatoes, skinned and sliced
Salt	Salt
Freshly ground black pepper	Freshly ground black pepper
1 × 200 g can sweetcorn kernels, drained	1 × 7 oz can sweetcorn kernels, drained
25 g plain flour	1 oz plain flour
150 ml milk	¼ pint milk
1 × 2.5 ml spoon made mustard	½ teaspoon made mustard
1 × 2.5 ml spoon dried basil	½ teaspoon dried basil
50 g mature Cheddar cheese, grated	2 oz mature Cheddar cheese, grated
3 eggs, separated	3 eggs, separated

Cooking Time: About 50 minutes
Oven: 180°C, 350°F, Gas Mark 4

Melt 25 g (1 oz) of the butter or margarine in a frying pan and fry the onion until soft and lightly browned. Add the tomatoes and cook for 1 to 2 minutes. Season well with salt and pepper. Put the sweetcorn into the bottom of a greased 15 cm (6 inch) soufflé or baking dish and spoon the onion mixture on top. Tie a piece of greased foil around the dish to come 5 cm (2 inches) above the rim.

Melt the remaining butter or margarine in a saucepan. Stir in the flour and cook for 1 minute. Gradually stir in the milk and bring to the boil. Simmer for 1 minute. Season well, then beat in the mustard, basil and cheese until melted, followed by the egg yolks. Beat the egg whites until stiff, then fold evenly through the sauce. Spoon into the dish and bake in a preheated moderate oven for 35 to 40 minutes or until well risen and well browned. Serve immediately.

Macaroni topkapi; Baked Spanish omelette; Orchard Cottage soufflé (front)

Cheese and tomato rarebits

Metric	Imperial	Cooking Time: 10 minutes
100 g mature Cheddar cheese, grated	4 oz mature Cheddar cheese, grated	Put the cheese, butter, salt and pepper to taste, mustard and Worcestershire sauce into a saucepan and heat very gently until melted. Stir in the flour and tomatoes. Spread the cheese mixture onto the toast and cook under a preheated moderate grill for about 5 minutes or until golden brown. Grill the bacon rashers at the same time and use to garnish the rarebits with the parsley. Serve hot.
15 g butter	½ oz butter	
Salt	Salt	
Black pepper	Black pepper	
1 × 5 ml spoon dry mustard	1 teaspoon dry mustard	
Dash of Worcestershire sauce	Dash of Worcestershire sauce	
1 × 15 ml spoon plain flour	1 tablespoon plain flour	
2 tomatoes, skinned and chopped	2 tomatoes, skinned and chopped	
2–4 slices of toast	2–4 slices of toast	
To garnish:	To garnish:	
4 streaky bacon rashers	4 streaky bacon rashers	
Fresh parsley sprigs	Fresh parsley sprigs	

Celery and ham au gratin

Metric	Imperial	
1 × 525 g can celery hearts	1 × 1 lb 3 oz can celery hearts	Cooking Time: 35 minutes
		Oven: 200°C, 400°F, Gas Mark 6
150 ml milk	¼ pint milk	Drain the celery, reserving 150 ml (¼ pint) of the can liquid. Mix the reserved liquid with the milk. Divide the celery into four even-sized portions. Melt the butter or margarine in a saucepan. Stir in the flour and cook for 1 minute. Gradually add the milk mixture and bring to the boil. Simmer for 1 minute. Season well with salt and pepper and stir in the cheese until melted.
25 g butter or margarine	1 oz butter or margarine	
25 g plain flour	1 oz plain flour	
Salt	Salt	
Black pepper	Black pepper	
50 g mature Cheddar cheese, grated	2 oz mature Cheddar cheese, grated	Cut the ham slices in half lengthways and wrap a piece around each piece of celery. Arrange in a greased shallow ovenproof dish. Pour the sauce over the rolls and sprinkle with a mixture of the Parmesan and breadcrumbs. Bake in a preheated moderately hot oven for about 30 minutes. Serve hot garnished with parsley.
2 slices of cooked ham	2 slices of cooked ham	
2 × 5 ml spoons grated Parmesan cheese	2 teaspoons grated Parmesan cheese	
1 × 15 ml spoon fresh breadcrumbs	1 tablespoon fresh breadcrumbs	
Fresh parsley sprigs to garnish	Fresh parsley sprigs to garnish	

Cauliflower with fluffy eggs

Metric	Imperial	Cooking Time: 20–25 minutes
1 small cauliflower, broken into florets	1 small cauliflower, broken into florets	Cook the cauliflower in boiling salted water until tender but still crisp. Meanwhile, melt the butter or margarine in a saucepan. Stir in the flour and cook for 1 minute. Gradually stir in the milk and bring to the boil, stirring frequently. Season well with salt and pepper, stir in the mustard and simmer for 2 minutes. Remove from the heat and stir in 75 g (3 oz) of the cheese until melted.
25 g butter or margarine	1 oz butter or margarine	
25 g plain flour	1 oz plain flour	
300 ml milk	½ pint milk	
Salt	Salt	
Freshly ground black pepper	Freshly ground black pepper	Drain the cauliflower very well, then divide between two shallow flameproof dishes. Pour over the sauce and cook under a preheated moderate grill for 3 to 4 minutes. Beat the egg whites until stiff, season with salt and pepper and pile on top of the cauliflower. Make two wells in the egg white. Drop an egg yolk into each well and sprinkle with the remaining cheese. Replace under the grill and cook until the meringue is lightly browned and the cheese melted. Serve sprinkled with paprika.
1 × 5 ml spoon made mustard	1 teaspoon made mustard	
100 g mature Cheddar cheese, grated	4 oz mature Cheddar cheese, grated	
2 large eggs, separated	2 large eggs, separated	
Paprika	Paprika	

Celery and ham au gratin; Cheese and tomato rarebits; Cauliflower with fluffy eggs

VEGETABLES AND SALADS

Vegetables are a very important part of our diet, providing vitamins and minerals and the roughage required for good digestion. It is worth bearing this in mind when cooking for two, as it often seems easier to take short cuts, or leave out vegetables and salads almost entirely. Remember, too, that freshly cooked vegetables and crisp salads make a meal more interesting, in flavour, texture and colour.

Fresh vegetables take longer to prepare and cook than frozen, but the result is worth the effort. You can take advantage of seasonal prices, too.

In cooking vegetables, whether fresh or frozen, be sure not to overcook them or they will be limp and tasteless. When they are tender, but still slightly crisp, drain and serve, topped with a knob of butter, pepper and perhaps some herbs.

Salads will probably feature more in planning meals for two than in an average family diet because of their ease and convenience. But be adventurous: mix chopped or grated raw vegetables such as leek, swede, celeriac or turnip into a mixed or green salad.

Mayonnaise

Metric

2 egg yolks
1 × 2.5 ml spoon dry mustard
1 × 2.5 ml spoon salt
1 × 2.5 ml spoon caster sugar
Large pinch of freshly ground pepper
300 ml salad oil
1–2 × 15 ml spoons lemon juice or wine vinegar

Imperial

2 egg yolks
½ teaspoon dry mustard
½ teaspoon salt
½ teaspoon caster sugar
Large pinch of freshly ground pepper
½ pint salad oil
1–2 tablespoons lemon juice or wine vinegar

All the ingredients must be at room temperature – a cold egg will cause curdling.

Put the egg yolks into a basin and beat in the mustard, salt, sugar and pepper. Gradually whisk in the oil a drop at a time until the sauce becomes thick and smooth. If the mayonnaise becomes too thick to whisk while adding the oil, add a little of the lemon juice or vinegar. Continue whisking in the oil in a thin steady stream. Add the remaining lemon juice or vinegar to taste. The mayonnaise may be kept in an airtight container in the refrigerator for 3 to 4 weeks.

Makes about 300 ml (½ pint)

Note: if the mayonnaise should curdle, put another egg yolk into a clean basin and very gradually whisk in the curdled sauce. Continue as before.

Stuffed aubergines

Metric	Imperial
1 × 15 ml spoon oil	*1 tablespoon oil*
1 garlic clove, crushed	*1 garlic clove, crushed*
1 onion, peeled and chopped	*1 onion, peeled and chopped*
1 large or 2 small aubergines	*1 large or 2 small aubergines*
50 g mushrooms, chopped	*2 oz mushrooms, chopped*
2 tomatoes, skinned and chopped	*2 tomatoes, skinned and chopped*
Salt	*Salt*
Freshly ground black pepper	*Freshly ground black pepper*
Good dash of Worcestershire sauce	*Good dash of Worcestershire sauce*
1 × 15 ml spoon chopped fresh parsley	*1 tablespoon chopped fresh parsley*
1 × 2.5–5 ml spoon chopped fresh thyme	*½–1 teaspoon chopped fresh thyme*
3 × 15 ml spoons fresh breadcrumbs	*3 tablespoons fresh breadcrumbs*
25 g Cheddar cheese, grated	*1 oz Cheddar cheese, grated*
Fresh parsley sprigs to garnish	*Fresh parsley sprigs to garnish*

Cooking Time: 45 minutes
Oven: 200°C, 400°F, Gas Mark 6

Heat the oil in a frying pan. Add the garlic and onion and fry until soft. Halve the aubergine(s) lengthways and cut out the flesh, leaving a thin layer inside the skin. Chop the flesh and add to the pan with the mushrooms. Cook for 4 to 5 minutes. Stir in the tomatoes, salt and pepper to taste, Worcestershire sauce and half the parsley. Spoon into the aubergine shells and arrange in an ovenproof dish.
Combine the remaining parsley, the thyme, breadcrumbs and cheese and sprinkle over the aubergines. Bake in a preheated moderately hot oven for about 30 minutes or until tender and the topping is browned. Garnish with parsley sprigs.

Stuffed aubergines

Scalloped potatoes

Metric

500 g potatoes, peeled and thinly sliced
1 large onion, peeled and thinly sliced
Salt
Freshly ground black pepper
50 g Cheddar cheese, grated (optional)
About 200 ml chicken stock
15 g butter or margarine
Chopped fresh parsley to garnish

Imperial

1 lb potatoes, peeled and thinly sliced
1 large onion, peeled and thinly sliced
Salt
Freshly ground black pepper
2 oz Cheddar cheese, grated (optional)
About ⅓ pint chicken stock
½ oz butter or margarine
Chopped fresh parsley to garnish

Cooking Time: About 1½ hours
Oven: 190°C, 375°F, Gas Mark 5

Layer the potatoes in a greased ovenproof dish with the onion, salt and pepper and most of the cheese (if used). Pour in sufficient stock to three-quarters fill the dish. Cover and bake in a preheated moderately hot oven for 45 minutes.

Remove the lid and sprinkle with the remaining cheese (if used) or with butter or margarine. Continue baking for a further 30 to 40 minutes or until the potatoes are tender and lightly browned. Serve hot, sprinkled with chopped parsley.

Leek and bacon tartlets

Metric

Pastry:
100 g plain flour
Pinch of salt
25 g butter or margarine
25 g lard or white fat
Water to mix

Filling:
15 g butter or margarine
1 medium leek, sliced
6 streaky bacon rashers, rinds removed, chopped
3 × 15 ml spoons cream
Salt
Freshly ground black pepper
40 g farmhouse Cheddar cheese, grated

Imperial

Pastry:
4 oz plain flour
Pinch of salt
1 oz butter or margarine
1 oz lard or white fat
Water to mix

Filling:
½ oz butter or margarine
1 medium leek, sliced
6 streaky bacon rashers, rinds removed, chopped
3 tablespoons cream
Salt
Freshly ground black pepper
1½ oz farmhouse Cheddar cheese, grated

Cooking Time: About 35 minutes
Oven: 220°C, 425°F, Gas Mark 7

Sift the flour and salt into a bowl. Rub in the fats until the mixture resembles breadcrumbs, then add sufficient water to mix to a pliable dough. Roll out the dough and use to line two 11–12 cm (4½–5 inch) individual tartlet tins or dishes. Bake blind in a preheated hot oven for about 15 minutes or until lightly browned.

Meanwhile melt the butter or margarine in a frying pan. Add the leek and fry until soft. Add the bacon and continue cooking for about 10 minutes or until the bacon is cooked and lightly browned. Stir in the cream, season well with salt and pepper and reheat gently. Spoon into the pastry cases and sprinkle with the cheese. Brown quickly under a preheated moderate grill. Serve hot.

Courgettes provençal

Metric

25 g butter or margarine
2 garlic cloves, crushed
1 onion, peeled and sliced
225 g courgettes, thinly sliced
2 large tomatoes, skinned and sliced
Salt
Freshly ground black pepper
25 g Cheddar cheese, finely grated
2 × 15 ml spoons fresh breadcrumbs

Imperial

1 oz butter or margarine
2 garlic cloves, crushed
1 onion, peeled and sliced
8 oz courgettes, thinly sliced
2 large tomatoes, skinned and sliced
Salt
Freshly ground black pepper
1 oz Cheddar cheese, finely grated
2 tablespoons fresh breadcrumbs

Cooking Time: About 20 minutes

Melt the butter or margarine in a frying pan. Add the garlic and onion and fry gently until lightly coloured. Add the courgettes and tomatoes, cover and cook gently, stirring occasionally, for about 10 minutes or until tender but still crisp. Season well with salt and pepper and pour into a flameproof dish. Sprinkle with a mixture of the cheese and breadcrumbs and brown quickly under a preheated hot grill.

Scalloped potatoes; Leek and bacon tartlets; Courgettes provençal

French bean, tomato and artichoke salad

French bean, tomato and artichoke salad

Metric

4–5 canned artichoke
hearts, drained
100 g French beans,
cooked and cut into 5 cm
pieces
2 × 5 ml spoons finely
chopped onion
3 × 15 ml spoons French
dressing
Salt
Black pepper
2 tomatoes, quartered
Lettuce leaves
Chopped fresh parsley

Imperial

4–5 canned artichoke
hearts, drained
4 oz French beans, cooked
and cut into 2 inch pieces
2 teaspoons finely chopped
onion
3 tablespoons French
dressing
Salt
Black pepper
2 tomatoes, quartered
Lettuce leaves
Chopped fresh parsley

Cut the artichoke hearts into halves or quarters and put into a bowl. Add the beans, onion, dressing and plenty of salt and pepper. Toss lightly and leave to stand for about 20 minutes.

Add the tomatoes. Arrange a bed of lettuce on a plate and spoon the salad into the centre. Sprinkle with chopped parsley and serve.

Celeriac and carrot salad

Metric

225 g celeriac, peeled and
coarsely grated
Juice of ½ lemon
2 large carrots, peeled and
coarsely grated
4 spring onions, sliced
2 × 15 ml spoons soured
cream
2 × 15 ml spoons thick
mayonnaise
1 × 2.5 ml spoon creamed
horseradish
Salt
Black pepper
Lettuce leaves

To garnish:
Black olives
Watercress sprigs

Imperial

8 oz celeriac, peeled and
coarsely grated
Juice of ½ lemon
2 large carrots, peeled and
coarsely grated
4 spring onions, sliced
2 tablespoons soured
cream
2 tablespoons thick
mayonnaise
½ teaspoon creamed
horseradish
Salt
Black pepper
Lettuce leaves

To garnish:
Black olives
Watercress sprigs

Put the celeriac into a bowl of cold water with the lemon juice. Leave to stand for 20 to 30 minutes. Drain very thoroughly and mix with the carrots and spring onions. Combine the soured cream, mayonnaise and horseradish with plenty of salt and pepper and fold through the vegetables. Serve the salad on a bed of lettuce garnished with black olives and watercress.

Red bean and tuna fish salad

Metric

2 green eating apples,
cored and thinly sliced
1 × 15 ml spoon lemon
juice
1 × 15 ml spoon finely
chopped onion
1 × 200 g can tuna fish,
drained and roughly
flaked
2.5 cm piece cucumber,
diced
Salt
Freshly ground black
pepper
4 × 15 ml spoons French
dressing
1 × 275 g can red kidney
beans, well drained

To garnish:
Watercress sprigs
1 hard-boiled egg

Imperial

2 green eating apples,
cored and thinly sliced
1 tablespoon lemon juice
1 tablespoon finely
chopped onion
1 × 7 oz can tuna fish,
drained and roughly
flaked
1 inch piece cucumber,
diced
Salt
Freshly ground black
pepper
4 tablespoons French
dressing
1 × 10 oz can red kidney
beans, well drained

To garnish:
Watercress sprigs
1 hard-boiled egg

Dip the apple slices quickly in lemon juice and put into a bowl with the onion, tuna fish, cucumber, plenty of salt and pepper and the dressing. Mix lightly and leave to stand for about 20 minutes.

Stir the beans into the salad. Arrange on two plates and garnish with sprigs of watercress around the edge and sliced, chopped or grated hard-boiled egg on top.

Red bean and tuna fish salad; Celeriac and carrot salad

Red cabbage and pineapple slaw

Metric

1 × 225 g can pineapple rings, drained and syrup reserved
2 × 15 ml spoons French dressing
Salt
Freshly ground black pepper
6 spring onions, sliced
25 g sultanas
175 g red cabbage, shredded
Few spring onions, chopped, to garnish

Imperial

1 × 8 oz can pineapple rings, drained and syrup reserved
2 tablespoons French dressing
Salt
Freshly ground black pepper
6 spring onions, sliced
1 oz sultanas
6 oz red cabbage, shredded
Few spring onions, chopped, to garnish

Reserve one pineapple ring for the garnish; chop the remainder and put into a bowl. Mix 1 × 15 ml spoon (1 tablespoon) of the reserved pineapple syrup with the dressing, season well with salt and pepper and add to the chopped pineapple with the spring onions, sultanas and cabbage. Toss well and serve in a bowl garnished with the pineapple ring and spring onions.

Red cabbage and pineapple slaw;
Courgette and mushroom salad

Courgette and mushroom salad

Metric	Imperial
100 g button mushrooms, sliced	4 oz button mushrooms, sliced
5 × 15 ml spoons French dressing	5 tablespoons French dressing
3 courgettes, thinly sliced	3 courgettes, thinly sliced
Salt	Salt
Freshly ground black pepper	Freshly ground black pepper
1 × 15 ml spoon chopped fresh parsley	1 tablespoon chopped fresh parsley
Few lettuce leaves	Few lettuce leaves

Put the mushrooms in a bowl with the dressing and mix well. Cover and leave to marinate for about 45 minutes, stirring occasionally. Meanwhile, cover the courgettes with boiling water, leave for 1 minute, then drain and plunge into cold water. Drain very thoroughly. Add to the mushrooms with plenty of salt and pepper. Toss well and marinate for a further 15 to 30 minutes. Stir in the parsley and serve on a bed of lettuce.

Salade niçoise

Metric	Imperial
Few lettuce leaves	Few lettuce leaves
100 g French or runner beans, cooked and cut into 4 cm pieces	4 oz French or runner beans, cooked and cut into 1½ inch pieces
1 potato, peeled, cooked and diced	1 potato, peeled, cooked and diced
3 spring onions, sliced, or 1 × 15 ml spoon chopped fresh chives	3 spring onions, sliced, or 1 tablespoon chopped fresh chives
1 small red pepper, cored, seeded and sliced	1 small red pepper, cored, seeded and sliced
1 × 90 g can tuna fish, drained and flaked	1 × 3½ oz can tuna fish, drained and flaked
½ × 50 g can anchovy fillets, drained and cut into thin strips	½ × 2 oz can anchovy fillets, drained and cut into thin strips
1 × 15 ml spoon capers	1 tablespoon capers
2 × 15 ml spoons French dressing	2 tablespoons French dressing

To garnish:	To garnish:
2 hard-boiled eggs, quartered	2 hard-boiled eggs, quartered
2 tomatoes, quartered	2 tomatoes, quartered
Few black olives	Few black olives

Arrange the lettuce in a bowl or on two individual plates. Mix together the beans, potato, onions or chives, red pepper, tuna fish, anchovies and capers. Add the dressing, toss lightly and spoon onto the lettuce. Garnish with wedges of egg, tomatoes and olives. Serve with hot crusty brown bread and butter.

Salade niçoise

FISH

When you decide on fish for dinner, you will find that there is plenty of scope for invention. Whichever fish you choose, there is a variety of ways to prepare it and different sauces to complement it.

Small whole fish are perfect when feeding two. Often with larger numbers of people, the grill pan will not accommodate all the fish in one batch.

Small whole plaice, trout, dab, lemon sole, whiting, etc. are all delicious grilled or pan fried and served with a savoury butter, butter sauce or simply lemon juice. They take only a few minutes to cook.

Many of the recipes here can also serve as a starter, either for 4 people by using the recipe as it is or by halving it for just the two of you.

Scallop kebabs

Metric

5–6 scallops
3 × 15 ml spoons oil
1 × 15 ml spoon vinegar
1 × 15 ml spoon lemon juice
Salt
Black pepper
1 × 2.5 ml spoon paprika
1 × 2.5 ml spoon dried basil
4 streaky bacon rashers, rinds removed, halved and rolled
25 g butter or margarine
50 g mushrooms, chopped
75 g peas, freshly cooked
75 g long-grain rice, freshly cooked

Imperial

5–6 scallops
3 tablespoons oil
1 tablespoon vinegar
1 tablespoon lemon juice
Salt
Black pepper
½ teaspoon paprika
½ teaspoon dried basil
4 streaky bacon rashers, rinds removed, halved and rolled
1 oz butter or margarine
2 oz mushrooms, chopped
3 oz peas, freshly cooked
3 oz long-grain rice, freshly cooked

Cooking Time: About 10 minutes

Cut each scallop into 2 to 3 pieces, depending on size. Mix the oil, vinegar, lemon juice, salt and pepper to taste, paprika and basil in a bowl. Add the scallops and leave to marinate for about 1 hour. Drain and thread onto long skewers alternating with bacon rolls. Cook under a pre-heated moderate grill for 8 to 10 minutes, turning several times and brushing with the marinade.

Melt the butter or margarine in a saucepan. Add the mushrooms and fry until soft. Stir in the peas and rice and season well. Spoon onto a warmed serving dish and top with the kebabs.

Scallop kebabs

Creamy scallops au gratin

Metric

5–6 scallops, cut into 2 cm pieces
4 × 15 ml spoons dry white wine
150 ml water
Salt
Freshly ground black pepper
25 g butter
1 small onion, peeled and finely chopped
2 × 15 ml spoons plain flour
2 × 5 ml spoons chopped fresh parsley
4 × 15 ml spoons single cream
350–500 g potatoes, cooked, peeled and mashed
25 g fresh breadcrumbs
40 g Cheddar cheese, grated
Fresh parsley sprigs to garnish

Imperial

5–6 scallops, cut into ¾ inch pieces
4 tablespoons dry white wine
¼ pint water
Salt
Freshly ground black pepper
1 oz butter
1 small onion, peeled and finely chopped
2 tablespoons plain flour
2 teaspoons chopped fresh parsley
4 tablespoons single cream
12 oz–1 lb potatoes, cooked, peeled and mashed
1 oz fresh breadcrumbs
1½ oz Cheddar cheese, grated
Fresh parsley sprigs to garnish

Cooking Time: About 20 minutes

Put the scallops into a saucepan and add the wine, water and salt and pepper to taste. Bring to the boil. Simmer gently for about 10 minutes or until tender. Strain and reserve 200ml (7 fl oz) of the liquor.

Melt the butter in another saucepan and fry the onion until soft. Stir in the flour and cook for 1 minute. Gradually stir in the reserved liquor and bring to the boil. Simmer for 2 minutes. Add the scallops, chopped parsley and cream, adjust the seasoning and reheat without boiling.

Meanwhile, pipe or spread the mashed potato around the edge of two individual shallow flameproof dishes or one larger dish. Brown under the grill. Spoon in the scallop mixture. Combine the breadcrumbs and cheese and sprinkle over the scallops. Lightly brown under a moderate grill and serve garnished with parsley.

Creamy scallops au gratin

Halibut with orange sauce; Oaty herrings with spicy mayonnaise; Stuffed mackerel

Halibut with orange sauce

Metric

2 halibut steaks
Juice of 1 lemon
2 egg yolks
2 × 15 ml spoons double
cream
5 × 15 ml spoons dry
white wine
Grated rind of ½ orange
Juice of 1 orange
Salt
Freshly ground black
pepper
Cayenne
65 g butter
15 g plain flour

To garnish:
Chopped fresh parsley
Orange slices

Imperial

2 halibut steaks
Juice of 1 lemon
2 egg yolks
2 tablespoons double
cream
5 tablespoons dry white
wine
Grated rind of ½ orange
Juice of 1 orange
Salt
Freshly ground black
pepper
Cayenne
2½ oz butter
½ oz plain flour

To garnish:
Chopped fresh parsley
Orange slices

Cooking Time: About 20 minutes

Sprinkle the halibut with half the lemon juice and leave in a cool place while making the sauce. Beat together the egg yolks, cream, wine, remaining lemon juice and orange rind and juice in a heatproof bowl. Stand over a pan of gently simmering water and heat gently, stirring, until the sauce is the consistency of thick pouring cream. Season to taste with salt, pepper and a pinch of cayenne, then beat in 25 g (1 oz) of the butter. Remove from the pan of water and keep warm.

Mix the flour with salt and pepper and use to coat the halibut. Melt the remaining butter in a frying pan. Add the fish and fry for about 5 minutes on each side or until browned and cooked through. Arrange the fish on a warmed serving dish, sprinkle with parsley and garnish with orange slices. Serve with the sauce.

Stuffed mackerel

Metric

2 small mackerel, cleaned
1 × 15 ml spoon chopped
onion
25 g fresh breadcrumbs
1 × 2.5 ml spoon finely
grated orange rind
½ eating apple, peeled,
cored and grated
1 × 5 ml spoon lemon juice
Salt
Freshly ground black
pepper
1 × 5 ml chopped fresh
chives
2 × 15 ml spoons orange
juice

To garnish:
Orange slices
Watercress sprigs

Imperial

2 small mackerel, cleaned
1 tablespoon chopped
onion
1 oz fresh breadcrumbs
½ teaspoon finely grated
orange rind
½ eating apple, peeled,
cored and grated
1 teaspoon lemon juice
Salt
Freshly ground black
pepper
1 teaspoon chopped fresh
chives
2 tablespoons orange juice

To garnish:
Orange slices
Watercress sprigs

Cooking Time: 25–30 minutes
Oven: 180°C, 350°F, Gas Mark 4

Cut the heads off the mackerel and remove the backbones (or ask your fishmonger to bone them for you). Wash and dry the fish. Mix together the onion, breadcrumbs, orange rind, apple, lemon juice, salt and pepper to taste and chives. Spread this stuffing inside the fish and roll up, securing with wooden cocktail sticks if necessary. Place in a well-greased ovenproof dish. Pour in the orange juice and cover with foil. Cook in a preheated moderate oven until the fish is cooked through. Garnish with slices of orange and watercress.

Note: To remove the backbone, split open along the stomach and lay on a flat surface, flesh side downwards. Press firmly along the backbone with your thumb, turn over and carefully ease out the loosened bones.

Oaty herrings with spicy mayonnaise

Metric

2 small herrings, boned
15 g plain flour
Salt
Freshly ground black
pepper
1 egg, beaten
50 g medium oatmeal or
porridge oats
25 g butter
1 × 15 ml spoon oil
Lemon wedges to garnish

Sauce:
4 × 15 ml spoons thick
mayonnaise
1 × 5 ml spoon
Worcestershire sauce
Grated rind of ½ small
lemon
1.5 × 5 ml spoons creamed
horseradish

Imperial

2 small herrings, boned
½ oz plain flour
Salt
Freshly ground black
pepper
1 egg, beaten
2 oz medium oatmeal or
porridge oats
1 oz butter
1 tablespoon oil
Lemon wedges to garnish

Sauce:
4 tablespoons thick
mayonnaise
1 teaspoon Worcestershire
sauce
Grated rind of ½ small
lemon
1½ teaspoons creamed
horseradish

Cooking Time: About 10 minutes

Cut each boned herring into two fillets. Mix the flour with salt and pepper and use to coat the herring fillets. Dip into beaten egg, then coat thoroughly with oatmeal or oats, pressing on well. Melt the butter with the oil in a frying pan and fry the herrings gently until browned on both sides – about 7 to 8 minutes.

Meanwhile combine all the ingredients for the sauce, adding salt and pepper to taste. Drain the herrings on absorbent kitchen paper. Garnish with lemon wedges and serve the sauce separately.

Smoked salmon flan

Metric

Pastry:
100 g plain flour
Pinch of salt
25 g butter or margarine
25 g lard or white fat
Water to mix

Filling:
100 g smoked salmon pieces
1 × 15 ml spoon chopped fresh chives or parsley
2 eggs
Salt
Freshly ground black pepper
150 ml single cream
3 × 15 ml spoons milk

Imperial

Pastry:
4 oz plain flour
Pinch of salt
1 oz butter or margarine
1 oz lard or white fat
Water to mix

Filling:
4 oz smoked salmon pieces
1 tablespoon chopped fresh chives or parsley
2 eggs
Salt
Freshly ground black pepper
¼ pint single cream
3 tablespoons milk

Cooking Time: 35-40 minutes
Oven: 220°C, 425°F, Gas Mark 7
180°C, 350°F, Gas Mark 4

Sift the flour and salt into a bowl. Rub in the fats until the mixture resembles fine breadcrumbs. Add sufficient water to mix to a pliable dough. Wrap and chill for 20 minutes, if possible. Roll out the dough and use to line a 15–17.5 cm (6–7 inch) flan ring or dish.

Chop the salmon and lay in the pastry case. Sprinkle with the chives or parsley. Beat together the eggs, salt and pepper, cream and milk and pour into the case. Bake in a preheated hot oven for 15 minutes, then reduce the temperature to moderate and continue baking for 20 to 25 minutes or until set and golden brown. Serve hot or cold.

Note: This can be made into 2 to 3 individual flans, using 11–12 cm (4½–5 inch) flan dishes.

Mixed fish risotto

Metric

25 g butter or margarine
1 onion, peeled and chopped
100 g long-grain rice
750 ml fish or chicken stock
1 × 2.5 ml spoon dried dill
Salt
Freshly ground black pepper
2 plaice fillets, skinned
50 g peeled prawns
50 g mushrooms, sliced
75 g peas, cooked

To garnish:
Strips of canned pimiento
Few bottled mussels

Imperial

1 oz butter or margarine
1 onion, peeled and chopped
4 oz long-grain rice
1¼ pints fish or chicken stock
½ teaspoon dried dill
Salt
Freshly ground black pepper
2 plaice fillets, skinned
2 oz peeled prawns
2 oz mushrooms, sliced
3 oz peas, cooked

To garnish:
Strips of canned pimiento
Few bottled mussels

Cooking Time: About 45 minutes

Melt the butter or margarine in a frying pan and fry the onion until soft. Add the rice and cook for 1 to 2 minutes, stirring well, then add the stock, dill and salt and pepper to taste. Bring to the boil. Cover and simmer for 20 minutes. Cut the fish into narrow strips and add to the pan with the prawns and mushrooms. Stir well, re-cover and continue simmering gently for a further 10 to 15 minutes, stirring occasionally and adding a little more boiling stock if necessary. Adjust the seasoning, stir in the peas and cook for a further 2 to 3 minutes. Serve garnished with strips of pimiento and mussels. Serve hot.

Moules marinière

Metric

2.3–2.8 l fresh mussels
50 g butter
1 onion, peeled and very finely chopped
300 ml white wine
Salt
Freshly ground black pepper
1 bouquet garni
2 × 5 ml spoons plain flour
1–2 × 15 ml spoons chopped fresh parsley

Imperial

4–5 pints fresh mussels
2 oz butter
1 onion, peeled and very finely chopped
½ pint white wine
Salt
Freshly ground black pepper
1 bouquet garni
2 teaspoons plain flour
1–2 tablespoons chopped fresh parsley

Cooking Time: 15 minutes

Wash the mussels very thoroughly, discarding any broken ones, scrubbing off mud and barnacles, and rinsing in several waters. Discard any mussels which do not close when given a sharp tap. Melt 40 g (1½ oz) of the butter in a saucepan and fry the onion until soft. Add the wine, salt and pepper to taste and bouquet garni and simmer for 2 minutes. Add the mussels, a few at a time, shaking well until all are added to the pan. Cover and simmer gently for 4 to 5 minutes or until the mussels are open. (Discard any which are still closed.) Place the mussels in a bowl and keep warm.

Mix together the remaining butter and the flour to make a paste and whisk into the juices in the pan. Adjust the seasoning, stir in the parsley and simmer for 2 minutes. Pour over the mussels and serve hot.

Mixed fish risotto; Moules marinière; Smoked salmon flan

Cod provençal; Crab gratiné; Cheese and prawn puffs

Cod provençal

Metric	Imperial
2 cod cutlets	2 cod cutlets
Salt	Salt
Freshly ground black pepper	Freshly ground black pepper
15 g butter or margarine	½ oz butter or margarine
Fresh parsley sprigs to garnish	Fresh parsley sprigs to garnish
Provençal sauce:	Provençal sauce:
1 × 15 ml spoon oil	1 tablespoon oil
50 g mushrooms, chopped	2 oz mushrooms, chopped
1 garlic clove, crushed	1 garlic clove, crushed
1 small onion, peeled and finely chopped	1 small onion, peeled and finely chopped
150 ml fish or chicken stock	¼ pint fish or chicken stock
4 × 15 ml spoons white wine or cider	4 tablespoons white wine or cider
1 × 5 ml spoon tomato purée	1 teaspoon tomato purée
1 bay leaf	1 bay leaf

Cooking Time: 15-20 minutes

Wipe the fish and season well with salt and pepper. Either grill, fry or poach, adding the butter or margarine, until tender.

Meanwhile, to make the sauce, heat the oil in a saucepan. Add the mushrooms, garlic and onion and fry until soft but not coloured. Add the stock, wine or cider, tomato purée, bay leaf and salt and pepper to taste and bring to the boil. Simmer uncovered for 10 to 15 minutes. Discard the bay leaf, adjust the seasoning and serve spooned over the fish. Garnish with parsley.

Note: This sauce can be used with all kinds of fish and shellfish, and with meats if chicken stock is used.

Cheese and prawn puffs

Metric	*Imperial*
20 g butter	¾ oz butter
4 × 15 ml spoons water	4 tablespoons water
25 g plain flour, sifted	1 oz plain flour, sifted
Salt	Salt
Freshly ground black pepper	Freshly ground black pepper
Cayenne pepper	Cayenne pepper
1 large egg, beaten	1 large egg, beaten
40 g mature Cheddar cheese, grated	1½ oz mature Cheddar cheese, grated
50 g peeled prawns, roughly chopped	2 oz peeled prawns, roughly chopped
Oil for deep frying	Oil for deep frying

Cocktail sauce:
3 × 15 ml spoons thick mayonnaise	3 tablespoons thick mayonnaise
2 × 15 ml spoons tomato ketchup	2 tablespoons tomato ketchup
Good dash of Worcestershire sauce	Good dash of Worcestershire sauce

To garnish:
Few unpeeled prawns	Few unpeeled prawns
Watercress sprigs	Watercress sprigs

Cooking Time: About 15 minutes

Melt the butter in the water gently in a saucepan, then bring to the boil. Add the flour all at once and beat well until smooth and the mixture leaves the sides of the pan clean. Remove from the heat. Season well with salt, pepper and cayenne and cool slightly. Beat in the egg, then the cheese and prawns.

Combine all the ingredients for the cocktail sauce and put in a small bowl. Heat the oil until a cube of bread browns in 20 seconds. Drop in teaspoonsful of the prawn mixture. Fry until golden brown all over. Drain well on absorbent kitchen paper and keep warm while frying the remainder. Serve the puffs hot, garnished with unpeeled prawns and watercress, with the cocktail sauce.

Crab gratiné

Metric	*Imperial*
25 g butter or margarine	1 oz butter or margarine
1 small onion, peeled and finely chopped	1 small onion, peeled and finely chopped
25 g plain flour	1 oz plain flour
250 ml milk	8 fl oz milk
Salt	Salt
Freshly ground black pepper	Freshly ground black pepper
Good pinch of dry mustard	Good pinch of dry mustard
2 × 5 ml spoons lemon juice	2 teaspoons lemon juice
50 g mushrooms, sliced	2 oz mushrooms, sliced
175–225 g crabmeat, flaked	6–8 oz crabmeat, flaked
25 g fresh breadcrumbs	1 oz fresh breadcrumbs
25 g Cheddar cheese, finely grated	1 oz Cheddar cheese, finely grated

To garnish:
Fresh parsley sprigs	Fresh parsley sprigs
Lemon twists	Lemon twists

Cooking Time: About 20 minutes

Melt the butter or margarine in a saucepan and fry the onion gently until soft but not coloured. Stir in the flour and cook for 1 minute. Gradually stir in the milk and bring to the boil. Season well with salt and pepper, add the mustard, lemon juice and mushrooms and simmer for 2 minutes. Stir in the crabmeat and cook for a further 2 minutes. Adjust the seasoning and spoon into one large or two individual flameproof dishes.

Combine the breadcrumbs and cheese and sprinkle over the crab. Cook under a preheated moderate grill until the topping is well browned. Serve garnished with parsley and lemon.

Prawns Newburg

Metric	Imperial
25 g butter or margarine	1 oz butter or margarine
100–175 g peeled prawns	4–6 oz peeled prawns
3 × 15 ml spoons Madeira or sweet sherry	3 tablespoons Madeira or sweet sherry
Salt	Salt
Freshly ground black pepper	Freshly ground black pepper
Paprika	Paprika
1 egg yolk	1 egg yolk
4 × 15 ml spoons single cream	4 tablespoons single cream
100 g long-grain rice, freshly cooked	4 oz long-grain rice, freshly cooked
1 × 15 ml spoon chopped fresh parsley	1 tablespoon chopped fresh parsley
Fresh parsley sprigs to garnish	Fresh parsley sprigs to garnish

Cooking Time: About 15 minutes

Melt the butter or margarine in a saucepan. Add the prawns and fry gently for 3 to 4 minutes. Stir in the Madeira or sherry and simmer gently for a further 3 to 4 minutes or until slightly reduced. Season well with salt, pepper and paprika. Beat the egg yolk into the cream and whisk gradually into the prawn mixture. Heat gently without boiling until slightly thickened and adjust the seasoning. Mix the rice and parsley and spoon onto two plates. Spoon the prawn mixture on top and garnish with parsley.

Prawns newburg; Cod cutlets celeste

Trout with mustard sauce

Trout with mustard sauce

Metric	Imperial
2 trout, cleaned	2 trout, cleaned
Salt	Salt
Freshly ground black pepper	Freshly ground black pepper
25 g butter	1 oz butter
1 × 15 ml spoon oil	1 tablespoon oil
2 × 15 ml spoons chopped onion	2 tablespoons chopped onion
6 × 15 ml spoons single cream	6 tablespoons single cream
1–2 × 5 ml spoons French mustard	1–2 teaspoons French mustard
1 × 5 ml spoon lemon juice	1 teaspoon lemon juice

To garnish:
Lemon slices
Chopped fresh parsley

To garnish:
Lemon slices
Chopped fresh parsley

Cooking Time: About 12 minutes

Wipe the fish and season the insides with salt and pepper. Melt the butter with the oil in a frying pan and fry the fish gently for about 5 minutes on each side or until cooked through. (The fish may be brushed with the oil and grilled if preferred.) Remove and keep warm.

Remove loose bits from the pan, then stir the onion into the remaining fat. Fry gently until soft. Add the cream, salt, pepper and mustard to taste and the lemon juice and heat gently for 2 to 3 minutes without boiling. Adjust the seasoning and pour over the fish. Dip the lemon slices into the parsley and use to garnish the fish.

Cod cutlets celeste

Metric	Imperial
2 cod cutlets	2 cod cutlets
Salt	Salt
Freshly ground black pepper	Freshly ground black pepper
1 small onion, peeled and finely chopped	1 small onion, peeled and finely chopped
1 garlic clove, crushed	1 garlic clove, crushed
15 g butter or margarine	½ oz butter or margarine
3 × 15 ml spoons cider	3 tablespoons cider
½ ripe avocado, peeled and stoned	½ ripe avocado, peeled and stoned
1 × 2.5 ml spoon lemon juice	½ teaspoon lemon juice
Finely grated rind of ¼ lemon	Finely grated rind of ¼ lemon

Cooking Time: About 35 minutes
Oven: 180°C, 350°F, Gas Mark 4

Season the fish well with salt and pepper and put into a lightly greased shallow ovenproof dish. Sprinkle with the onion and garlic and dot with the butter or margarine. Pour over the cider and cover the dish with foil. Cook in a preheated moderate oven for about 30 minutes or until tender.

Mash most of the avocado until smooth. Strain off the cooking liquor from the fish and beat into the avocado together with the lemon juice and rind and salt and pepper to taste. Put into a saucepan and bring slowly to the boil, stirring continuously.

Serve the fish with the avocado sauce spooned over and garnished with the remaining avocado, cut into thin slices.

43

Clockwise: Buttered trout with almonds; Haddock varma; Quick sardine and tomato pizza; Fish pie

Fish pie

Metric

225 g cod or haddock fillet
6 × 15 ml spoons dry cider
Salt
Black pepper
Milk
1 canned pimiento,
chopped
1 × 5 ml spoon dried dill
1 hard-boiled egg,
chopped
1 × 15 ml spoon chopped
fresh parsley
20 g butter or margarine
20 g plain flour
350 g potatoes, cooked,
peeled and mashed
25 g Cheddar cheese,
grated

Imperial

8 oz cod or haddock fillet
6 tablespoons dry cider
Salt
Black pepper
Milk
1 canned pimiento,
chopped
1 teaspoon dried dill
1 hard-boiled egg,
chopped
1 tablespoon chopped
fresh parsley
¾ oz butter or margarine
¾ oz plain flour
12 oz potatoes, cooked,
peeled and mashed
1 oz Cheddar cheese,
grated

Cooking Time: 45 minutes
Oven: 190°C, 375°F, Gas Mark 5

Poach the fish in the cider with salt and pepper to taste for about 10 minutes or until tender. Drain, reserving the liquor, and make it up to 200 ml (7 fl oz) with milk. Flake the fish and mix with the pimiento, dill, egg and parsley. Melt the butter or margerine in a saucepan. Stir in the flour and cook for 1 minute. Gradually stir in the liquor mixture and bring to the boil. Simmer for 2 minutes. Season well, then stir in the fish mixture. Pour into an ovenproof dish. Pipe the mashed potato around the edge and sprinkle with the grated cheese. Bake in a preheated moderately hot oven for about 30 minutes or until lightly browned on top.

Note: This dish can be made the day before and refrigerated until required.

Haddock varma

Metric	Imperial
350 g haddock fillet, skinned	12 oz haddock fillet, skinned
Salt	Salt
Freshly ground black pepper	Freshly ground black pepper
1 × 15 ml spoon chopped onion	1 tablespoon chopped onion
2 tomatoes, skinned and chopped	2 tomatoes, skinned and chopped
1 × 15 ml spoon tomato purée	1 tablespoon tomato purée
1 garlic clove, crushed (optional)	1 garlic clove, crushed (optional)
2 × 5 ml spoons lemon juice	2 teaspoons lemon juice
3–4 × 15 ml spoons white wine or cider	3–4 tablespoons white wine or cider
40 g fresh breadcrumbs	1½ oz fresh breadcrumbs

Cooking Time: 35–40 minutes
Oven: 200°C, 400°F, Gas Mark 6

Lay the haddock in a buttered ovenproof dish and season well with salt and pepper. Combine the onion, tomatoes, tomato purée, garlic (if used), lemon juice and wine or cider and spoon over the fish. Sprinkle with the breadcrumbs and cook in a preheated moderately hot oven until cooked through and the topping is browned.

Quick sardine and tomato pizza

Metric	Imperial
100 g self-raising flour	4 oz self-raising flour
Salt	Salt
Freshly ground black pepper	Freshly ground black pepper
50 g butter or margarine	2 oz butter or margarine
2 × 5 ml spoons dried mixed herbs	2 teaspoons dried mixed herbs
1 egg, beaten	1 egg, beaten
Milk	Milk
1 onion, peeled and sliced	1 onion, peeled and sliced
2 tomatoes, skinned and sliced	2 tomatoes, skinned and sliced
1 × 125 g can sardines in tomato sauce	1 × 4 oz can sardines in tomato sauce
50–75 g Mozarella cheese, sliced	2–3 oz Mozarella cheese, sliced
Fresh parsley sprigs to garnish	Fresh parsley sprigs to garnish

Cooking Time: 20–25 minutes
Oven: 230°C, 450°F, Gas Mark 8

Sift the flour into a bowl with salt and pepper to taste. Rub in 25 g (1 oz) of the butter or margarine until the mixture resembles fine breadcrumbs. Add the herbs, egg and sufficient milk to mix to a softish dough. Shape into a 15 cm (6 inch) round on a greased baking sheet.

Melt the remaining butter in a frying pan and add the onion. Fry until soft and spoon over the dough. Arrange the tomatoes on the onion. Arrange the sardines on top with the juices from the can and cover with the cheese. Bake in a preheated very hot oven for 15 to 20 minutes or until well risen and the cheese is lightly browned. Serve hot garnished with parsley.

Buttered trout with almonds

Metric	Imperial
2 trout, cleaned	2 trout, cleaned
Salt	Salt
Freshly ground black pepper	Freshly ground black pepper
3 × 15 ml spoons lemon juice	3 tablespoons lemon juice
50 g butter	2 oz butter
40 g flaked almonds	1½ oz flaked almonds
Watercress sprigs to garnish	Watercress sprigs to garnish

Cooking Time: About 10 minutes

Wipe the trout and season lightly with salt and pepper. Put into a foil-lined grill pan, pour over 1 × 15 ml spoon (1 tablespoon) of the lemon juice and dot with 15 g (½ oz) of the butter. Cook under a moderate heat for about 4 to 5 minutes on each side or until cooked through.

Meanwhile, melt the remaining butter in a small frying pan and fry the almonds gently until light brown. Remove from the heat and quickly stir in the remaining lemon juice. Reheat gently, adjust the seasoning and spoon over the trout. Garnish with watercress.

POULTRY AND MEAT

It is easy to plan a main dish for two nowadays, because butchers and supermarkets offer the smaller cuts and joints of meat and poultry. You can buy portions of duck, cuts and portions of turkey and chicken, small whole or half birds and small roasting joints specially prepared for two people, as well as the usual chops, steaks, escalopes and stewing meat.

The recipes given here make use of these smaller cuts and joints, and many of them are very quick to prepare. Cidered drumsticks, Chicken fries, Turkey à l'orange, Beef and peanut burgers, Lamb noisettes, and Veal Marsala are just a few examples. There are also dishes using cooked poultry and meat, should you have any leftovers from a larger bird or joint. These include Chicken and ham pies, Curried chicken and rice salad, Lamb samosa and Ham and mushroom gougère.

Coq au vin blanc

Coq au vin blanc

Metric	Imperial
25 g butter	1 oz butter
1 × 15 ml spoon oil	1 tablespoon oil
1 × 2.5 cm thick streaky bacon slice, rind removed, chopped	1 × 1 inch thick streaky bacon slice, rind removed, chopped
100 g button onions, peeled	4 oz button onions, peeled
1 garlic clove, crushed	1 garlic clove, crushed
½ small chicken	½ small chicken
200 ml dry white wine	7 fl oz dry white wine
150 ml chicken stock	¼ pint chicken stock
1 bouquet garni	1 bouquet garni
Large pinch of dried mixed herbs	Large pinch of dried mixed herbs
Salt	Salt
Freshly ground black pepper	Freshly ground black pepper
50 g button mushrooms	2 oz button mushrooms
15 g plain flour	½ oz plain flour

Cooking Time: $1\frac{1}{4}$–$1\frac{1}{2}$ hours
Oven: 170°C, 325°F, Gas Mark 3

Melt 15 g (½ oz) of the butter with the oil in a frying pan. Add the bacon and fry until golden brown. Transfer the bacon to a flameproof casserole. Fry the onions and garlic in the pan until lightly browned and add to the casserole. Cut the chicken in half or into four pieces and put in the pan. Brown on all sides, then add to the casserole.

Remove excess fat from the frying pan. Stir in the wine and stock and bring to the boil. Pour into the casserole and add the bouquet garni, herbs and salt and pepper to taste. Cover tightly. Cook in a preheated warm oven for about 1 hour.

Add the mushrooms and continue cooking for 15 minutes. Discard the bouquet garni. Cream the remaining butter and the flour together and whisk this beurre manié gradually into the casserole. Bring to the boil on top of the stove. Adjust the seasoning and serve with parsleyed new potatoes.

Cidered chicken drumsticks

Metric	Imperial
25 g plain flour	1 oz plain flour
Salt	Salt
Freshly ground black pepper	Freshly ground black pepper
4 chicken drumsticks	4 chicken drumsticks
25 g butter or margarine	1 oz butter or margarine
1 onion, peeled and sliced	1 onion, peeled and sliced
150 ml medium cider	¼ pint medium cider
3 × 15 ml spoons chicken stock	3 tablespoons chicken stock
50 g button mushrooms, sliced	2 oz button mushrooms, sliced
8 black olives	8 black olives
2 × 15 ml spoons double cream	2 tablespoons double cream
Chopped fresh parsley to garnish	Chopped fresh parsley to garnish

Cooking Time: 35-40 minutes

Mix the flour with salt and pepper and use to coat the chicken. Melt the butter or margarine in a saucepan and fry the onion until browned. Remove from the pan. Add the chicken and fry gently until well browned all over. Return the onion to the pan and stir in the cider, stock and salt and pepper to taste. Bring to the boil. Cover and simmer gently for 15 minutes.

Add the mushrooms and olives and continue to cook, turning the chicken occasionally, for a further 10 to 15 minutes or until tender. Stir in the cream, adjust the seasoning and reheat gently. Serve sprinkled with parsley.

Cucumbered chicken

Metric	Imperial
2 chicken portions or 4 chicken thighs	2 chicken portions or 4 chicken thighs
Salt	Salt
Black pepper	Black pepper
25 g butter or margarine	1 oz butter or margarine
1 onion, peeled and sliced	1 onion, peeled and sliced
3 streaky bacon rashers, rinds removed, thopped	3 streaky bacon rashers, rinds removed, chopped
1.5 × 15 ml spoons plain flour	1½ tablespoons plain flour
300 ml chicken stock	½ pint chicken stock
1 × 15 ml spoon lemon juice	1 tablespoon lemon juice
12.5 cm piece cucumber, diced	5 inch piece cucumber, diced

Cooking Time: About 1 hour
Oven: 180°C, 350°F, Gas Mark 4

Rub the chicken with salt and pepper. Melt the butter or margarine in a frying pan. Add the chicken and fry until well browned all over. Remove from the pan. Fry the onion and bacon in the pan until lightly browned. Stir in the flour and cook for 1 minute, then gradually stir in the stock. Bring to the boil, stirring. Season to taste with salt and pepper and add the lemon juice. Replace the chicken in the pan.

Add the cucumber to the pan, cover and simmer gently for about 30 minutes or until the chicken is tender. Alternatively, transfer to a casserole and cook in a preheated moderate oven for 30 to 40 minutes. Adjust the seasoning and serve.

Chicken Lucinda

Metric	Imperial
2 chicken breasts, boned	2 chicken breasts, boned
Salt	Salt
Freshly ground black pepper	Freshly ground black pepper
2 small slices of cooked ham	2 small slices of cooked ham
25 g butter	1 oz butter
1 onion, peeled and sliced	1 onion, peeled and sliced
1 × 15 ml spoon plain flour	1 tablespoon plain flour
200 ml chicken stock	7 fl oz chicken stock
2 × 5 ml spoons tomato purée	2 teaspoons tomato purée
1 × 225 g can tomatoes	1 × 8 oz can tomatoes
1 × 2.5 ml spoon Angostura bitters	½ teaspoon Angostura bitters

Cooking Time: 45 minutes
Oven: 180°C, 350°F, Gas Mark 4

Beat the chicken well, then season with salt and pepper and lay a piece of ham on each breast. Wrap the chicken around the ham and secure with wooden cocktail sticks. Melt the butter in a frying pan. Add the chicken and fry until browned. Transfer to a small ovenproof casserole.

Fry the onion in the pan until soft. Stir in the flour and cook for 1 minute, then gradually stir in the stock, tomato purée and tomatoes with the can juice. Bring to the boil, season well with salt and pepper and add the bitters. Pour over the chicken in the casserole. Cover and cook in a preheated oven for about 40 minutes or until tender.

Note: A mixture of red wine and stock can be used for this recipe.

Chicken Lucinda; Cucumbered chicken; Cidered chicken drumsticks; Pot roast chicken

Pot roast chicken

Metric

1 × 15 ml spoon dripping
1 onion, peeled and sliced
2 carrots, peeled and sliced
1 courgette, sliced
Salt
Freshly ground black pepper
1 × 5 ml spoon dried mixed herbs
1 × 1–1.25 kg oven-ready chicken
150 ml cider or chicken stock .

Imperial

1 tablespoon dripping
1 onion, peeled and sliced
2 carrots, peeled and sliced
1 courgette, sliced
Salt
Freshly ground black pepper
1 teaspoon dried mixed herbs
1 × 2–2½ lb oven-ready chicken
¼ pint cider or chicken stock

Cooking Time: About 1 hour
Oven: 180°C, 350°F, Gas Mark 4

There will be some chicken left over, unless you are very hungry. Use the chicken to make Chicken and ham pies. Heat the dripping in a flameproof casserole. Add the onion and carrots and fry until soft but not brown. Lay the courgette on the vegetables, season well with salt and pepper and sprinkle on the herbs. Season the chicken and place on the vegetables, pushing it well down. Pour the cider or stock over the chicken. Cover and cook in a preheated moderate oven for 30 minutes. Baste the chicken and continue cooking for 15 minutes. Remove the lid and continue cooking for about 15 minutes, basting frequently, or until the chicken is tender and lightly browned. Serve on a dish surrounded by the vegetables and with the cooking juices as a sauce.

49

Chicken fries with curry dip; Chicken and ham pies; Curried chicken and rice salad

Chicken fries with curry dip

Metric

2 chicken breasts
About 25 g plain flour
Salt
Freshly ground black
pepper
1 egg, beaten
Golden breadcrumbs
Oil for deep frying

Curry dip:
2 × 15 ml spoons
mayonnaise
2 × 15 ml spoons soured
cream
1 × 5 ml spoon curry
powder
Large dash of
Worcestershire sauce
8 stuffed green olives,
chopped
2 × 5 ml spoons chopped
fresh chives or spring
onion tops

To garnish:
Tomato wedges
Mustard and cress

Imperial

2 chicken breasts
About 1 oz plain flour
Salt
Freshly ground black
pepper
1 egg, beaten
Golden breadcrumbs
Oil for deep frying

Curry dip:
2 tablespoons mayonnaise
2 tablespoons soured
cream
1 teaspoon curry powder
Large dash of
Worcestershire sauce
8 stuffed green olives,
chopped
2 teaspoons chopped fresh
chives or spring onion tops

To garnish:
Tomato wedges
Mustard and cress

Cooking Time: About 15 minutes

Cut the chicken into narrow strips about 4 cm (1½ inches) long. Mix the flour with salt and pepper and use to coat the chicken pieces. Dip in the beaten egg, then in the breadcrumbs, coating well. Chill until ready to cook.

To make the dip, combine all the ingredients with salt and pepper to taste and put into a small dish in the centre of a plate.

Heat oil in a deep frying pan until a cube of bread will brown in 30 seconds. Fry the chicken strips until golden brown and cooked through. Drain well on absorbent kitchen paper. Pile the chicken fries around the dip and garnish with tomatoes and cress.

Chicken and ham pies

Metric	Imperial
15 g butter or margarine	½ oz butter or margarine
15 g plain flour	½ oz plain flour
6 × 15 ml spoons milk	6 tablespoons milk
Salt	Salt
Freshly ground black pepper	Freshly ground black pepper
1 × 2.5 ml spoon dried tarragon (optional)	½ teaspoon dried tarragon (optional)
40 g cooked ham, chopped	1½ oz cooked ham, chopped
75 g cooked chicken meat, chopped	3 oz cooked chicken meat, chopped
2 hard-boiled eggs	2 hard-boiled eggs

Pastry:	Pastry:
175 g plain flour	6 oz plain flour
Pinch of salt	Pinch of salt
40 g butter or margarine	1½ oz butter or margarine
40 g lard or white fat	1½ oz lard or white fat
Water to mix	Water to mix
Beaten egg or milk to glaze	Beaten egg or milk to glaze

Cooking Time: About 35 minutes
Oven: 220°C, 425°F, Gas Mark 7

Melt the butter or margarine in a saucepan. Stir in the flour and cook for 1 minute, then gradually stir in the milk. Bring to the boil, stirring continuously, and simmer for 2 minutes. Remove from the heat and stir in salt and pepper to taste, the tarragon (if used), ham and chicken. Leave to cool.

To make the pastry, sift the flour and salt into a bowl. Rub in the fats until the mixture resembles breadcrumbs. Add sufficient water to mix to a pliable dough. Roll out the dough and cut out two 12 cm (5 inch) rounds and two 17cm (6½ inch) rounds. Place the small rounds on a baking sheet. Divide the filling between the small rounds, leaving a plain margin all around the edge. Bury an egg in each pile of filling. Dampen the dough edges and carefully cover with the large rounds of dough. Press the edges well together and crimp. Decorate the tops with the dough trimmings and make a hole in the centres. Brush all over with egg or milk. Bake in a preheated hot oven for 25 to 30 minutes or until golden brown. Serve hot or cold.

Curried chicken and rice salad

Metric	Imperial
100 g long-grain rice	4 oz long-grain rice
4 × 15 ml spoons thick mayonnaise	4 tablespoons thick mayonnaise
2 × 15 ml spoons lemon juice	2 tablespoons lemon juice
1 × 5 ml spoon curry powder	1 teaspoon curry powder
1 × 15 ml spoon chopped fresh chives or spring onions	1 tablespoon chopped fresh chives or spring onions
Salt	Salt
Freshly ground black pepper	Freshly ground black pepper
1 red eating apple, cored and sliced	1 red eating apple, cored and sliced
½ green pepper, cored, seeded, chopped and blanched	½ green pepper, cored, seeded, chopped and blanched
50 g raisins or sultanas	2 oz raisins or sultanas
175 g cooked chicken meat, diced	6 oz cooked chicken meat, diced
25 g flaked almonds, toasted	1 oz flaked almonds, toasted
Watercress sprigs to garnish	Watercress sprigs to garnish

Cook the rice in boiling salted water until just tender – about 12 minutes. Rinse, drain well and cool. Combine the mayonnaise, 1 × 15 ml spoon (1 tablespoon) of the lemon juice, the curry powder, chives or spring onions and salt and pepper to taste. Dip the apple slices in the remaining lemon juice, then add to the mayonnaise mixture with the green pepper, raisins or sultanas and chicken. Fold through the rice and adjust the seasoning. Serve on a flat dish, sprinkled with almonds and garnished with watercress.

Duck with black cherries

Metric	Imperial
2 duck portions	2 duck portions
Salt	Salt
Freshly ground black pepper	Freshly ground black pepper
1 × 425 g can black cherries	1 × 15 oz can black cherries
Grated rind of ½ orange	Grated rind of ½ orange
Juice of 1 orange	Juice of 1 orange
1 × 5 ml spoon cornflour	1 teaspoon cornflour
1 × 15 ml spoon water	1 tablespoon water
To garnish:	To garnish:
Watercress sprigs	Watercress sprigs
Orange slices	Orange slices

Cooking Time: About 50 minutes
Oven: 200°C, 400°F, Gas Mark 6

Trim the duck, season well with salt and pepper and prick the skin all over with a fork. Put into a lightly greased ovenproof dish or tin and roast in a preheated hot oven for 10 minutes.

Drain the cherries and measure 150 ml (¼ pint) syrup. Add the orange rind and juice to the cherry syrup, season well and pour over the duck. Return to the oven and roast for 20 minutes, basting several times with the juices. Add half the cherries and continue to cook, still basting regularly, for about 10 minutes or until the duck is tender.

Transfer the duck to a warmed serving plate. Keep hot. Skim the fat from the cooking juices and pour into a saucepan. Dissolve the cornflour in the water and add to the pan. Bring to the boil, stirring. Adjust the seasoning and simmer until thickened. Pour over the duck. Garnish with watercress and orange slices.

Note: Use the remaining cherries to serve with ice cream.

Turkey à l'orange

Metric	Imperial
1 orange	1 orange
25 g butter or margarine	1 oz butter or margarine
1 onion, peeled and sliced	1 onion, peeled and sliced
225 g turkey meat (thigh or breast), cubed	8 oz turkey meat (thigh or breast), cubed
50 g mushrooms, sliced	2 oz mushrooms, sliced
1 × 225 g can tomatoes, drained	1 × 8 oz can tomatoes, drained
4 × 15 ml spoons orange juice	4 tablespoons orange juice
Salt	Salt
Freshly ground black pepper	Freshly ground black pepper

Cooking Time: About 30 minutes

Finely pare the rind from half the orange and cut into julienne strips. Blanch in boiling water for about 10 minutes or until tender. Drain well. Grate the remaining orange rind.

Melt the butter or margarine in a saucepan and fry the onion until lightly coloured. Add the turkey and continue cooking for about 5 minutes or until evenly browned. Stir in the mushrooms and cook for 2 minutes, stirring frequently. Add the tomatoes, grated orange rind and juice and salt and pepper to taste and bring to the boil. Cover and simmer for about 20 minutes or until the turkey is tender and the juices well reduced and thickened. Adjust the seasoning and serve on a bed of rice sprinkled with the orange rind strips.

Roast partridges

Metric	Imperial
2 partridges, oven-ready	2 partridges, oven-ready
25 g butter	1 oz butter
Salt	Salt
Freshly ground black pepper	Freshly ground black pepper
3–4 streaky bacon rashers	3–4 streaky bacon rashers
2 × 15 ml spoons dripping	2 tablespoons dripping
1 × 15 ml spoon plain flour	1 tablespoon plain flour
To serve:	To serve:
2 pieces of fried bread	2 pieces of fried bread
Watercress sprigs	Watercress sprigs

Cooking Time: 30–40 minutes
Oven: 230°C, 450°F, Gas Mark 8
    200°C, 400°F, Gas Mark 6

Wipe the birds and put half the butter inside each. Season lightly with salt and pepper, cover the breasts with the bacon and truss. Heat the dripping in a roasting tin. Put in the birds and turn to coat with the dripping. Roast in a preheated very hot oven for 10 minutes. Reduce the oven to moderately hot and continue roasting for 20 to 30 minutes, depending on size, basting frequently. Remove the bacon and dredge the breasts lightly with the flour. Baste with the fat in the tin and return to the oven to cook for 5 minutes. Serve on fried bread with a thin gravy made from the pan drippings. Garnish with watercress sprigs. Traditional accompaniments are fried crumbs and bread sauce.

Note: To fry crumbs melt 25 g (1 oz) butter in a pan. Add 4 × 15 ml spoons (4 tablespoons) fresh breadcrumbs and fry until golden brown, stirring continuously.

Duck with black cherries; Roast partridges; Turkey à l'orange

Turkey mozzarella

Metric	Imperial
225 g boned turkey breast	8 oz boned turkey breast
Salt	Salt
Freshly ground black pepper	Freshly ground black pepper
25 g plain flour	1 oz plain flour
25 g butter or margarine	1 oz butter or margarine
100 g button mushrooms, sliced	4 oz button mushrooms, sliced
4 × 15 ml spoons chicken stock	4 tablespoons chicken stock
75 g Mozzarella cheese, sliced	3 oz Mozzarella cheese, sliced
Chopped fresh herbs to garnish	Chopped fresh herbs to garnish

Cooking Time: About 25 minutes

Beat the turkey flat and cut into 4 to 6 pieces. Season well with salt and pepper and coat evenly with the flour. Melt the butter or margarine in a frying pan and fry the turkey until golden brown all over and cooked through – about 15 minutes. Transfer to a shallow flameproof dish and keep warm.

Fry the mushrooms in the pan for 3 to 4 minutes, then spoon over the turkey. Add the stock and salt and pepper to taste to the pan and boil until reduced by half. Pour over the turkey. Lay the slices of cheese on top and put under a preheated moderate grill. Cook until the cheese is melted and lightly browned. Serve hot, garnished with fresh herbs.

Duck with Cumberland sauce

Metric	Imperial
2 duck portions	2 duck portions
Salt	Salt
Freshly ground black pepper	Freshly ground black pepper
1 × 5 ml spoon oil	1 teaspoon oil
Sauce:	Sauce:
1 × 5 ml spoon coarsely grated orange rind	1 teaspoon coarsely grated orange rind
2 × 15 ml spoons redcurrant jelly	2 tablespoons redcurrant jelly
120 ml port or red wine	4 fl oz port or red wine
Juice of 1 orange	Juice of 1 orange
1 × 15 ml spoon lemon juice	1 tablespoon lemon juice
To garnish:	To garnish:
Fresh parsley sprigs	Fresh parsley sprigs
Apple slices	Apple slices

Cooking Time: About 50 minutes
Oven: 220°C, 425°F, Gas Mark 7

Trim the duck, season well with salt and pepper and prick all over with a fork. Place in a roasting tin and brush lightly with the oil. Roast in a preheated hot oven for about 45 minutes, basting twice, or until tender and the skin is crispy.

Meanwhile, blanch the orange rind in boiling water for 3 minutes and drain. Mix the rind with the redcurrant jelly, port or wine and orange and lemon juices. Transfer the duck to a warmed serving dish and keep warm. Skim the fat from the pan drippings and stir in the sauce mixture. Heat gently to melt the jelly, then boil for 1 to 2 minutes. Adjust the seasoning and pour over the duck. Garnish with parsley and apple slices.

Turkey mozzarella; Duck with Cumberland sauce

Pot roast garlic chicken

Metric	Imperial
½ packet sage and onion stuffing mix	½ packet sage and onion stuffing mix
1 × 15 ml spoon chopped fresh parsley	1 tablespoon chopped fresh parsley
Salt	Salt
Freshly ground black pepper	Freshly ground black pepper
100 g garlic sausage	4 oz garlic sausage
1 × 1.25–1.5 kg oven-ready chicken	1 × 2½–3 lb oven-ready chicken
2 × 15 ml spoons dripping or 25 g butter	2 tablespoons dripping or 1 oz butter
1 large onion, peeled and sliced	1 large onion, peeled and sliced
150 ml dry white wine	¼ pint dry white wine
Fresh parsley sprigs to garnish	Fresh parsley sprigs to garnish

Cooking Time: About 1–1¼ hours
Oven: 180°C, 350°F, Gas Mark 4

There will be leftovers from this, unless you manage to eat it all. Serve cold the next day.

Make up the stuffing mix following the directions on the packet, then mix in the parsley and salt and pepper to taste. Chop half the garlic sausage and add to the stuffing. Leave to cool, then use to stuff the neck end of the chicken. Put any surplus stuffing in the cavity. Truss the bird.

Melt the dripping or butter in a frying pan and lightly brown the bird all over. Transfer to a large ovenproof casserole and season well. Fry the onion in the pan until lightly coloured, then add the wine and bring to the boil. Slice the remaining garlic sausage and add to the pan. Stir well and pour the mixture over and around the chicken.

Cover and cook in a preheated moderate oven for about 1 hour or until the chicken is tender. Remove the lid and continue cooking for 5 minutes. Remove the chicken from the casserole and carve. Serve with the onion mixture and juices in the casserole, garnished with parsley.

Pot roast garlic chicken

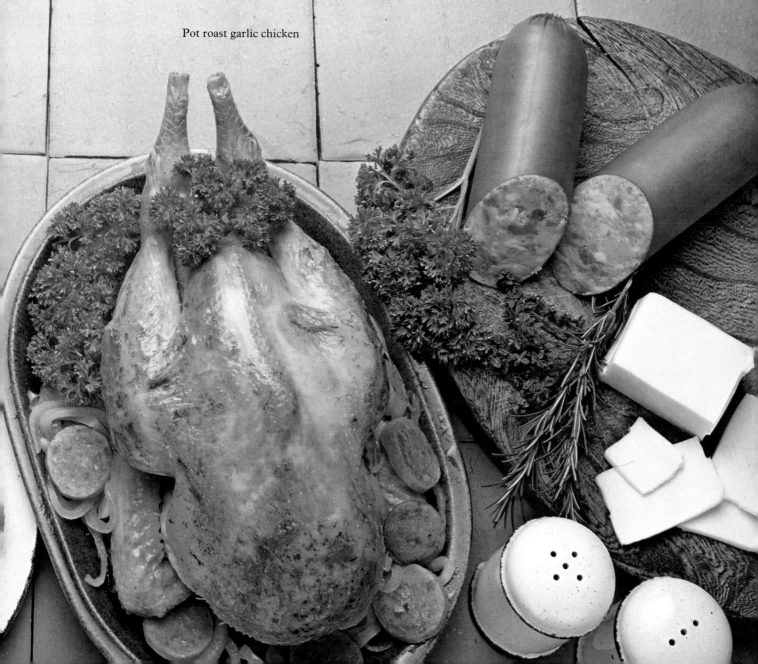

Grouse à l'americaine

Metric	Imperial
1 young grouse	*1 young grouse*
25 g butter, melted	*1 oz butter, melted*
Salt	*Salt*
Freshly ground black pepper	*Freshly ground black pepper*
50 g fresh white breadcrumbs	*2 oz fresh white breadcrumbs*
Paprika	*Paprika*
6 streaky bacon rashers, rinds removed, rolled	*6 streaky bacon rashers, rinds removed, rolled*
2 tomatoes, halved	*2 tomatoes, halved*

To garnish:
Game chips
Watercress sprigs
Lemon wedges

To garnish:
Game chips
Watercress sprigs
Lemon wedges

Cooking Time: 35–50 minutes
Oven: 220°C, 425°F, Gas Mark 7

Cut the grouse open down the back and flatten. Brush the flesh side liberally with melted butter and season all over with salt and pepper. Put into a grill pan and cook under a preheated moderate grill for 10 minutes. (Alternatively, cook in a preheated hot oven for the same cooking time.) Sprinkle all over with the breadcrumbs and season lightly with paprika. Continue to cook for about 20 to 30 minutes or until tender and cooked through. Cook the bacon rolls and tomatoes alongside the grouse for the last 15 minutes. Serve garnished with game chips, watercress sprigs and lemon wedges and use the pan drippings and a little stock to make a thin gravy. Bread sauce can also be served.

Pheasant Normandy-style

Pheasant Normandy-style

Metric

25 g butter
1 small pheasant
1 onion, peeled and
chopped
2 × 15 ml spoons
Calvados or brandy
(optional)
2 cooking apples, peeled,
cored and sliced
Finely grated rind of ½
lemon
Salt
Freshly ground black
pepper
6 × 15 ml spoons single
cream

To garnish:
Watercress sprigs
Bacon rolls, cooked

Imperial

1 oz butter
1 small pheasant
1 onion, peeled and
chopped
2 tablespoons Calvados or
brandy (optional)
2 cooking apples, peeled,
cored and sliced
Finely grated rind of ½
lemon
Salt
Freshly ground black
pepper
6 tablespoons single cream

To garnish:
Watercress sprigs
Bacon rolls, cooked

Cooking Time: About 1 hour
Oven: 180°C, 350°F, Gas Mark 4

Melt the butter in a frying pan and brown the pheasant all over. Place in a deep ovenproof casserole. Fry the onion in the pan until soft. Add the Calvados or brandy, if used, and the apples. Cook for 1 to 2 minutes, then stir in the lemon rind, salt and pepper to taste and the cream. Mix lightly and spoon around the pheasant. Cover the casserole tightly and cook in a preheated moderate oven for about 1 hour or until tender.

Arrange the pheasant on a warmed serving dish with the apple mixture around the edge and garnish with watercress and bacon rolls.

57

Flemish beef

Metric	Imperial
1 × 15 ml spoon dripping	1 tablespoon dripping
350 g stewing or braising steak, cut into 2.5 cm cubes	12 oz stewing or braising steak, cut into 1 inch cubes
1 large onion, peeled and sliced	1 large onion, peeled and sliced
1 garlic clove, crushed	1 garlic clove, crushed
2 streaky bacon rashers, rinds removed, chopped	2 streaky bacon rashers, rinds removed , chopped
300 ml brown ale	½ pint brown ale
Salt	Salt
Freshly ground black pepper	Freshly ground black pepper
Pinch of grated nutmeg	Pinch of grated nutmeg
1 bay leaf	1 bay leaf
1 × 5 ml spoon vinegar	1 teaspoon vinegar
1 × 5 ml spoon sugar	1 teaspoon sugar
2 carrots, peeled and sliced	2 carrots, peeled and sliced
2–3 × 5 ml spoons cornflour dissolved in 2 × 15 ml spoons water (optional)	2–3 teaspoons cornflour dissoved in 2 tablespoons water (optional)
Few fried mushrooms to garnish	Few fried mushrooms to garnish

Cooking Time: About 1¾ hours
Oven: 180°C, 350°F, Gas Mark 4

Heat the dripping in a frying pan and brown the meat all over. Transfer to an ovenproof casserole. Fry the onion, garlic and bacon in the pan until golden brown. Drain off any excess fat in the pan, then stir in the ale, plenty of salt and pepper, the nutmeg, bay leaf, vinegar, sugar and carrots. Bring to the boil, then add to the casserole and stir well. Cover tightly. Cook in a preheated moderate oven for about 1½ hours or until the meat is tender.

Discard the bay leaf. If you like, thicken the liquid with the dissolved cornflour. Adjust the seasoning and garnish with mushrooms.

Beef and peanut burgers

Metric	Imperial
40 g salted peanuts	1½ oz salted peanuts
225 g lean minced beef	8 oz lean minced beef
1 × 15 ml spoon chopped onion	1 tablespoon chopped onion
Salt	Salt
Freshly ground black pepper	Freshly ground black pepper
1 egg yolk	1 egg yolk
2 × 15 ml spoons oil	2 tablespoons oil
2 baps, split	2 baps, split
2 tomatoes, sliced	2 tomatoes, sliced

Cooking Time: 5-10 minutes

Chop most of the peanuts, leaving a few for garnish. Combine the mince, onion, chopped peanuts and plenty of salt and pepper and bind together with the egg yolk. Divide in two and shape into flat round cakes. Heat the oil in a frying pan and fry the burgers for about 5 minutes on each side or until lightly browned and cooked through. Serve in warmed baps, topped with sliced tomatoes and a few whole peanuts. Accompany with a salad.

Whisky steaks

Metric	Imperial
2 steaks (fillet, sirloin or rump)	2 steaks (fillet, sirloin or rump)
Salt	Salt
Freshly ground black pepper	Freshly ground black pepper
25 g butter	1 oz butter
1 garlic clove, crushed	1 garlic clove, crushed
4 × 15 ml spoons whisky	4 tablespoons whisky
1 × 5 ml spoon Worcestershire sauce	1 teaspoon Worcestershire sauce
Chopped fresh chives to garnish	Chopped fresh chives to garnish

Cooking Time: 8–15 minutes

Trim the steaks and season well with salt and pepper. Melt the butter in a frying pan and fry the garlic until soft. Add the steaks and fry quickly to seal on both sides. Continue to cook for 2 to 6 minutes or until cooked to your taste. Add the whisky and Worcestershire sauce and bring to the boil. Adjust the seasoning and serve sprinkled with chives.

Note: Whisky may be replaced by medium sherry.

Beef and peanut burgers; Flemish beef; Whisky steaks

Steak Cristobelle

Metric	Imperial
2 quick-fry steaks	2 quick-fry steaks
Salt	Salt
Freshly ground black pepper	Freshly ground black pepper
25 g butter or margarine	1 oz butter or margarine
½ garlic clove, halved	½ garlic clove, halved
1 onion, peeled and sliced	1 onion, peeled and sliced
½ red pepper, cored, seeded and sliced	½ red pepper, cored, seeded and sliced
50 g mushrooms, sliced	2 oz mushrooms, sliced
2 × 15 ml spoons red wine	2 tablespoons red wine
1 × 5 ml spoon Worcestershire sauce	1 teaspoon Worcestershire sauce
1 × 5 ml spoon French mustard	1 teaspoon French mustard

Cooking Time: About 10 minutes

Trim the steaks and season well with salt and pepper. Melt the butter or margarine in a frying pan. Add the garlic and fry for 1 minute, then remove. Add the onion to the pan and fry gently until soft. Add the red pepper and mushrooms and continue cooking until soft and the onion is lightly coloured. Push the vegetables to the side of the pan and add the steaks. Cook quickly to seal on both sides, then lower the heat and spread the vegetables over the meat. Add the wine, Worcestershire sauce, mustard and salt and pepper to taste. Cook gently for 4 to 5 minutes or until the steak is cooked to your liking. Serve at once.

Lamb noisettes with herb butter; Thatched lamb and aubergine pie

Steak Cristobelle

Thatched lamb and aubergine pie

Metric	Imperial
15 g butter or margarine	½ oz butter or margarine
1 small onion, peeled and chopped	1 small onion, peeled and chopped
1 garlic clove, crushed	1 garlic clove, crushed
225 g lean minced lamb	8 oz lean minced lamb
2 × 5 ml spoons plain flour	2 teaspoons plain flour
1 × 225 g can tomatoes	1 × 8 oz can tomatoes
1 × 15 ml spoon tomato purée	1 tablespoon tomato purée
4–6 × 15 ml spoons stock	4–6 tablespoons stock
Salt	Salt
Black pepper	Black pepper
1 small aubergine, chopped	1 small aubergine, chopped
350 g potatoes, peeled, cooked and mashed	12 oz potatoes, peeled, cooked and mashed

Cooking Time: 35–40 minutes

Melt the butter or margarine in a frying pan and fry the onion and garlic until lightly browned. Stir in the minced lamb and cook slowly for 10 minutes, stirring frequently. Add the flour and cook for 1 minute, then add the tomatoes with the can juice, tomato purée, stock and salt and pepper to taste. Bring slowly to the boil. Add the aubergine, cover and simmer gently for about 20 minutes, adding a little more stock if necessary to prevent sticking, until tender and thick. Adjust the seasoning and pour into a flameproof dish. Pipe the potato over the top in a lattice pattern. Brown under a preheated hot grill.

Lamb noisettes with herb butter

Metric	Imperial
75 g butter	3 oz butter
Salt	Salt
Black pepper	Black pepper
½ garlic clove, crushed	½ garlic clove, crushed
1 × 2.5 ml spoon grated lemon rind	½ teaspoon grated lemon rind
1 × 15 ml spoon chopped fresh herbs (e.g. parsley, thyme, fennel)	1 tablespoon chopped fresh herbs (e.g. parsley, thyme, fennel)
2–4 lamb noisettes	2–4 lamb noisettes
2–4 slices of toast, cut into rounds	2–4 slices of toast, cut into rounds
150 ml beef stock	¼ pint beef stock
To garnish:	To garnish:
Fresh parsley sprigs	Fresh parsley sprigs
Grilled tomatoes	Grilled tomatoes

Cooking Time: About 20 minutes

Soften 50g (2 oz) of the butter in a bowl and beat in salt and pepper to taste, the garlic, lemon rind and herbs. Shape into a block, wrap in greaseproof paper or foil and chill.

Season the noisettes with salt and pepper. Melt the remaining butter in a frying pan. Add the noisettes, cover and fry for 5 to 8 minutes. Turn over and continue frying for a further 5 to 8 minutes or until cooked through. Remove from the pan and put each noisette on a toast round. Keep warm.

Stir the stock into the pan drippings. Season well and boil rapidly until reduced to about 3 × 15 ml spoons (3 tablespoons). Spoon over the noisettes. Top each with slices of the herb butter and garnish with sprigs of fresh herbs and tomatoes.

Pork fillet en croute; Pork chops with barbecue sauce; Marinated pork kebabs

Pork chops with barbecue sauce

Metric

1 onion, peeled
1 garlic clove, crushed
1.5 × 15 ml spoons
tarragon vinegar
2 × 5 ml spoons
Worcestershire sauce
25 g brown sugar
Grated rind and juice of ½
lemon
Large pinch of chilli
powder
Salt
5 × 15 ml spoons water
2 large pork chops
Freshly ground black
pepper
Orange or lemon slices to
garnish

Imperial

1 onion, peeled
1 garlic clove, crushed
1½ tablespoons tarragon
vinegar
2 teaspoons
Worcestershire sauce
1 oz brown sugar
Grated rind and juice of ½
lemon
Large pinch of chilli
powder
Salt
5 tablespoons water
2 large pork chops
Freshly ground black
pepper
Orange or lemon slices to
garnish

Cooking Time: About 25 minutes

Finely chop the onion and put into a saucepan with the garlic, vinegar, Worcestershire sauce, brown sugar, lemon rind and juice and chilli powder, *or* put all the ingredients mentioned into a blender and blend until smooth, then turn into a saucepan. Add 1 × 5 ml spoon (1 teaspoon) salt and the water and bring to the boil. Simmer gently, uncovered, for 15 minutes, stirring occasionally, or until the onion is tender and the sauce slightly thickened.

Meanwhile, trim the chops, season lightly with salt and pepper and put on a grill rack. Cook under a preheated moderate grill for about 8 to 10 minutes on each side or until cooked through and well browned. Serve with the sauce spooned over and garnished with orange or lemon slices.

Note: This sauce is fairly hot so use it sparingly.

Pork fillet en croûte

Metric	Imperial
1 pork fillet (about 225 g)	1 pork fillet (about 8 oz)
Salt	Salt
Freshly ground black pepper	Freshly ground black pepper
1 × 2.5 ml spoon dried sage	½ teaspoon dried sage
4–6 streaky bacon rashers, rinds removed	4–6 streaky bacon rashers, rinds removed
1 × 15 ml spoon oil	1 tablespoon oil
175 g frozen puff pastry, thawed	6 oz frozen puff pastry, thawed
Little beaten egg	Little beaten egg
Parsley sprigs to garnish	Parsley sprigs to garnish
Mushroom sauce:	Mushroom sauce:
25 g butter or margarine	1 oz butter or margarine
50 g mushrooms, chopped	2 oz mushrooms, chopped
20 g plain flour	¾ oz plain flour
300 ml chicken stock	½ pint chicken stock
Pinch of ground mace	Pinch of ground mace

Cooking Time: 50–60 minutes
Oven: 220°C, 425°F, Gas Mark 7
    180°C, 350°F, Gas Mark 4

Trim the fillet, cut in half and put one piece on top of the other. Season lightly with salt and pepper and sprinkle with sage. Wrap the bacon around the pork and secure with wooden cocktail sticks, if necessary. Heat the oil in a frying pan. Add the pork and brown it all over for about 10 minutes. Remove and cool. Roll out the pastry dough thinly. Place the pork in the centre and wrap the dough around to enclose completely. Dampen the edges and press well together to seal. Place on a dampened baking sheet, seam underneath, and decorate with the dough trimmings. Glaze with the beaten egg and cook in a preheated hot oven for 15 minutes. Reduce the heat to moderate and continue cooking for 20 to 25 minutes.

Just before the pork is ready, make the sauce. Melt the butter or margarine in a saucepan and fry the mushrooms for 2 to 3 minutes. Stir in the flour and cook for 1 minute. Gradually stir in the stock and bring to the boil. Simmer for 2 to 3 minutes. Season to taste with salt and pepper, add the mace and serve with the pork, cut into slices. Garnish with parsley.

Marinated pork kebabs

Metric	Imperial
2 × 15 ml spoons wine vinegar	2 tablespoons wine vinegar
1 × 5 ml spoon made mustard	1 teaspoon made mustard
Salt	Salt
Freshly ground black pepper	Freshly ground black pepper
1–2 × 15 ml spoons soy sauce	1–2 tablespoons soy sauce
2 × 15 ml spoons oil	2 tablespoons oil
1 × 15 ml spoon finely chopped onion	1 tablespoon finely chopped onion
1 large pork fillet or 350 g lean leg of pork, cubed	1 large pork fillet or 12 oz lean leg of pork, cubed
1 green pepper, cored, seeded and cut into small pieces	1 green pepper, cored, seeded and cut into small pieces

Cooking Time: 15-20 minutes

Mix together the vinegar, mustard, salt and pepper to taste, soy sauce, oil and onion in a bowl. Add the pork cubes and allow to marinate for 1 to 2 hours, turning several times. Remove the pork from the marinade and thread onto two long skewers, alternating with pieces of green pepper. Cook under a preheated moderate grill for 5 to 8 minutes on each side or until cooked through and well browned, basting with the marinade several times during cooking. Serve on a bed of savoury rice.

Veal Marsala

Metric	Imperial
2 veal escalopes	2 veal escalopes
Salt	Salt
Freshly ground black pepper	Freshly ground black pepper
25 g butter	1 oz butter
4 × 15 ml spoons Marsala	4 tablespoons Marsala
1–2 × 5 ml spoons lemon juice	1–2 teaspoons lemon juice
To garnish:	To garnish:
Lemon slices	Lemon slices
Chopped fresh parsley	Chopped fresh parsley
Triangles of fried bread	Triangles of fried bread

Cooking Time: 10-15 minutes

Trim the veal and season lightly with salt and pepper. Melt the butter in a frying pan and when foaming add the escalopes. Cook for 3 to 4 minutes on each side or until lightly browned and almost cooked through. Pour the Marsala over the veal and add the lemon juice and salt and pepper to taste. Cook gently for a few minutes, turning the veal at least once. Adjust the seasoning and serve hot, garnished with lemon slices dipped in chopped parsley and triangles of fried bread.

Lemon veal with paprika

Metric	Imperial
1 × 15 ml spoon oil	1 tablespoon oil
2 streaky bacon rashers, rinds removed, chopped	2 streaky bacon rashers, rinds removed, chopped
1 onion, peeled and sliced	1 onion, peeled and sliced
300 g lean pie veal, cubed	10 oz lean pie veal, cubed
200 ml chicken stock	7 fl oz chicken stock
2 × 5 ml spoons paprika	2 teaspoons paprika
Grated rind and juice of ½ lemon	Grated rind and juice of ½ lemon
Salt	Salt
Freshly ground black pepper	Freshly ground black pepper
4 × 15 ml spoons soured cream	4 tablespoons soured cream
25g flaked almonds, toasted, to garnish	1 oz flaked almonds, toasted, to garnish

Cooking Time: About 1¼ hours
Oven: 180°C, 350°F, Gas Mark 4

Heat the oil in a frying pan and fry the bacon and onion until lightly browned. Drain and place in an ovenproof casserole. Add the veal cubes to the pan and brown all over. Add to the casserole. Heat the stock, paprika, lemon rind and juice and salt and pepper in a saucepan and pour into the casserole. Cover tightly and cook in a preheated moderate oven for about 1 hour or until the veal is tender. Stir in the soured cream, adjust the seasoning and reheat gently. Serve sprinkled with almonds.

Creamed veal

Metric	Imperial
15 g butter	½ oz butter
1 × 15 ml spoon oil	1 tablespoon oil
225-350 g lean veal (fillet or leg), cut into thin strips	8–12 oz lean veal (fillet or leg), cut into thin strips
1 onion, peeled and finely chopped	1 onion, peeled and finely chopped
100 g mushrooms, sliced	4 oz mushrooms, sliced
Salt	Salt
Freshly ground black pepper	Freshly ground black pepper
4–6 × 15 ml spoons double cream	4–6 tablespoons double cream
2 × 15 ml spoons chopped fresh parsley	2 tablespoons chopped fresh parsley
2 × 5 ml spoons chopped fresh mint	2 teaspoons chopped fresh mint

Cooking Time: About 10 minutes

Melt the butter with the oil in a frying pan and fry the veal until well sealed and lightly browned. Remove from the pan. Fry the onion in the pan until soft. Add the mushrooms and continue cooking for 2 to 3 minutes. Return the veal to the pan, season well with salt and pepper and cook gently for 2 to 3 minutes. Stir in the cream and most of the parsley and mint and heat gently, stirring continuously. Adjust the seasoning and serve on a bed of rice, sprinkled with the remaining parsley and mint.

Lemon veal with paprika; Creamed veal; Veal Marsala

Ham and mushroom gougère

Metric

40 g butter
100 ml water
50 g plain flour, sifted
1 large egg

Filling:
25 g butter or margarine
1 small onion, peeled and sliced
1 small green pepper, cored, seeded and chopped
50 g mushrooms, sliced
15 g plain flour
4 × 15 ml spoons cider
4–6 × 15 ml spoons milk
Salt
Freshly ground black pepper
Pinch of dry mustard
175 g cooked ham, chopped
25 g Cheddar cheese, grated

Imperial

1½ oz butter
3½ fl oz water
2 oz plain flour, sifted
1 large egg

Filling:
1 oz butter or margarine
1 small onion, peeled and sliced
1 small green pepper, cored, seeded and chopped
2 oz mushrooms, sliced
½ oz plain flour
4 tablespoons cider
4–6 tablespoons milk
Salt
Freshly ground black pepper
Pinch of dry mustard
6 oz cooked ham, chopped
1 oz Cheddar cheese, grated

Cooking Time: About 35 minutes
Oven: 220°C, 425°F, Gas Mark 7

For the gougère, put the butter and water into a saucepan and bring to the boil. Stir in the flour all at once and beat well until the mixture leaves the sides of the pan clean. Cool slightly, then beat in the egg. Spread or pipe the mixture into a 15 cm (6 inch) ring, making sure the ends meet, on a greased baking sheet. Bake in a preheated hot oven for about 30 minutes or until well risen, golden brown and firm.

Meanwhile, make the filling. Melt the butter or margarine in a saucepan and fry the onion and green pepper gently until soft. Add the mushrooms and continue cooking for 2 to 3 minutes. Stir in the flour and cook for 1 minute, then gradually stir in the cider, milk, salt and pepper to taste and mustard. Bring to the boil, stirring continuously. Add the ham and simmer gently for 2 minutes.

Cut off the top one-third of the gougère and scoop out any soggy dough. Spoon in the filling, replace the lid and sprinkle with the cheese. Return to the oven to bake for 3 to 4 minutes to melt the cheese. Serve hot.

Veal ragusa

Metric

2 × 15 ml spoons oil
1 onion, peeled and finely chopped
1 garlic clove, crushed
1 small red pepper, cored, seeded and chopped
1 × 15 ml spoon tomato purée
1 × 225 g can tomatoes
Salt
Freshly ground black pepper
2 × 5 ml spoons lemon juice
2 veal escalopes
1 small egg, beaten
Fresh white breadcrumbs
25 g butter

To garnish:
Lemon slices
Black olives

Imperial

2 tablespoons oil
1 onion, peeled and finely chopped
1 garlic clove, crushed
1 small red pepper, cored, seeded and chopped
1 tablespoon tomato purée
1 × 8 oz can tomatoes
Salt
Freshly ground black pepper
2 teaspoons lemon juice
2 veal escalopes
1 small egg, beaten
Fresh white breadcrumbs
1 oz butter

To garnish:
Lemon slices
Black olives

Cooking Time: 20-25 minutes

Heat 1 × 15 ml spoon (1 tablespoon) of the oil in a saucepan and fry the onion and garlic until soft. Add the red pepper and continue cooking for 5 minutes. Stir in the tomato purée, tomatoes with the can juice, salt and pepper to taste and lemon juice. Bring to the boil, cover and simmer very gently, stirring occasionally, for about 15 minutes or until thick.

Meanwhile season the veal with salt and pepper. Dip in the beaten egg, then coat in the breadcrumbs. Chill for 20 minutes. Fry in a mixture of the remaining oil and the butter for 3 to 5 minutes on each side, or until cooked through and golden brown. Drain on absorbent kitchen paper. Spoon the sauce over the meat, and garnish with lemon slices and black olives.

Bacon chops with plum sauce; Ham and mushroom gougère; Veal ragusa

Bacon chops with plum sauce

Metric

*2 lean bacon chops (about
2.5 cm thick), rind
removed*
75 g plum jam
*2 × 15 ml spoons wine
vinegar*
2 × 15 ml spoons water
*1 × 5 ml spoon dry
mustard*
Salt
*Freshly ground black
pepper*
*Large pinch of dried
mixed herbs*
*Watercress sprigs to
garnish*

Imperial

*2 lean bacon chops (about
1 inch thick), rind
removed*
3 oz plum jam
*2 tablespoons wine
vinegar*
2 tablespoons water
1 teaspoon dry mustard
Salt
*Freshly ground black
pepper*
*Large pinch of dried
mixed herbs*
*Watercress sprigs to
garnish*

Cooking Time: 10–15 minutes

Make deep slashes in the fat of the chops to prevent curling
up during cooking. Grill under a preheated moderate grill
for 4 to 5 minutes on each side or until the fat is well
browned.

Meanwhile, make the sauce. Put all the remaining
ingredients with salt and pepper to taste into a small pan
and heat gently, stirring continuously, until well blended.
Bring to the boil and simmer for 2 minutes. Serve the sauce
spooned over the chops and garnished with watercress.

DESSERTS

Often with only two people, you will be tempted just to end a meal with cheese and biscuits or fresh fruit. But when a dessert is called for, the recipes here will provide the answer. They are quick to prepare and many can be made in advance.

You will find something for every occasion, formal or informal, and to suit all palates. And you will see that with only a little extra time and thought, a dessert can be prepared to end a meal in the true sense.

Chocolate rum pots

Metric	Imperial
50 g plain chocolate	2 oz plain chocolate
15 g butter	½ oz butter
2 egg yolks	2 egg yolks
1 × 15 ml spoon rum	1 tablespoon rum
1 large egg white	1 large egg white

To decorate:	To decorate:
3 × 15 ml spoons whipping cream	3 tablespoons whipping cream
Few pistachio nuts or walnuts, chopped	Few pistachio nuts or walnuts, chopped

Cooking Time: 3-4 minutes

Break up the chocolate and put into a heatproof bowl over a pan of hot water or in the top of a double saucepan. Add the butter and heat gently until melted and smooth. Remove from the heat and beat in the egg yolks and rum. Beat the egg white until stiff and fold evenly through the chocolate mixture. Divide between two individual dishes or glasses and chill. Just before serving, whip the cream until stiff and use to decorate the tops. Sprinkle with chopped nuts.

Pears with port and orange sauce

Metric	Imperial
6 × 15 ml spoons port or red wine	6 tablespoons port or red wine
Grated rind of 1 orange	Grated rind of 1 orange
4 × 15 ml spoons orange juice	4 tablespoons orange juice
4 × 15 ml spoons water	4 tablespoons water
3 × 15 ml spoons sugar	3 tablespoons sugar
2 firm pears	2 firm pears

Cooking Time: 15 minutes

Put the port or wine, orange rind and juice and water in a saucepan and bring to the boil. Add the sugar and stir to dissolve. Peel the pears carefully, leaving the wooden stalk intact. Add the pears to the pan and simmer gently, basting frequently, until just tender but not mushy – about 10 minutes.

Transfer the pears to a serving dish. Boil the sauce rapidly until syrupy and reduced by about half. Pour the sauce over the pears and leave to cool. Chill thoroughly and serve with whipped cream.

Note: Hard pears, such as Conference, will take longer to cook than the softer varieties.

Chocolate rum pots; Pears with port and orange sauce; Marrons crèmes

Marrons crèmes

Metric

*2 × 15 ml spoons
sweetened chestnut purée
1 × 15 ml spoon coffee
liqueur or brandy
150 ml double or
whipping cream
3–4 marrons glacés
1 egg white*

Imperial

*2 tablespoons sweetened
chestnut purée
1 tablespoon coffee
liqueur or brandy
¼ pint double or whipping
cream
3–4 marrons glacés
1 egg white*

Mix together the chestnut purée and liqueur or brandy. Whip the cream until thick but not too stiff and mix three quarters of it into the chestnut mixture. Chop 2 to 3 marrons glacés and stir into the chestnut mixture. Beat the egg white until very stiff and fold evenly through the mixture. Spoon into two serving glasses and chill, if you like.

Whip the remaining cream until stiff and pipe a whirl on top of each serving. Decorate with a halved marron glacé and serve with sponge fingers.

69

Syllabub

Metric	Imperial
1 large egg white	*1 large egg white*
50 g caster sugar	*2 oz caster sugar*
Large pinch of finely grated lemon rind	*Large pinch of finely grated lemon rind*
2 × 5 ml spoons lemon juice	*2 teaspoons lemon juice*
4 × 15 ml spoons dry white wine	*4 tablespoons dry white wine*
150 ml double cream	*¼ pint double cream*
Lemon slices to decorate	*Lemon slices to decorate*

Beat the egg white until very stiff. Fold in the caster sugar, lemon rind and juice and wine. Whip the cream until thick but not too stiff and fold evenly through the mixture. Spoon into two tall glasses and leave to stand in a cool place for several hours to allow the mixture to separate. Decorate with lemon twists and serve with langue de chat biscuits.
Note: Dry cider can be used in place of white wine.

Ginger cream trifle

Metric	Imperial
3 trifle sponge cakes	*3 trifle sponge cakes*
1 × 225 g can apricot halves, drained (syrup reserved) and halved	*1 × 8 oz can apricot halves, drained (syrup reserved) and halved*
3–4 pieces stem ginger in syrup, chopped	*3–4 pieces stem ginger in syrup, chopped*
150 ml double or whipping cream	*¼ pint double or whipping cream*
Few flaked almonds, toasted	*Few flaked almonds, toasted*
Candied angelica	*Candied angelica*

Cut the sponge cakes into small pieces. Reserve five apricot pieces for decoration and mix the remainder with the cake and the ginger in a serving dish. Mix 2 × 15 ml spoons (2 tablespoons) of ginger syrup with 3 × 15 ml spoons (3 tablespoons) of the apricot syrup and spoon over the apricot mixture. Whip the cream until thick but not stiff and spoon over the trifle. Decorate with the reserved apricots, toasted almonds and strips of angelica.

Minted grapefruit sorbet

Metric

75 g sugar
200 ml water
1 fresh mint sprig
1 × 15 ml spoon finely
grated grapefruit rind
150 ml grapefruit juice
1 egg white

Imperial

3 oz sugar
7 fl oz water
1 fresh mint sprig
1 tablespoon finely grated
grapefruit rind
¼ pint grapefruit juice
1 egg white

Cooking Time: 5 minutes

Dissolve the sugar in the water in a saucepan. Add the sprig of mint and bring to the boil. Boil rapidly for 5 minutes, then allow to cool thoroughly. Remove the mint and stir in the grapefruit rind and strained juice. Pour into an ice tray or shallow dish and freeze until granular.

Turn into a bowl and beat well. Beat the egg white until stiff and fold evenly through the mixture. Return to the ice tray and freeze until firm. Serve spooned into glasses or cleaned grapefruit shells.

Custard ice cream

Metric

200 ml milk
1 × 15 ml spoon custard
powder
2 × 15 ml spoons sugar
1 × 2.5 ml spoon vanilla
essence
150 ml double cream
1 egg white
Few fresh raspberries
(optional)

Imperial

7 fl oz milk
1 tablespoon custard
powder
2 tablespoons sugar
½ teaspoon vanilla essence
¼ pint double cream
1 egg white
Few fresh raspberries
(optional)

Cooking Time: 5 minutes

Heat most of milk to almost boiling. Mix the custard powder with the remaining milk, then stir into the hot milk. Bring to the boil slowly, stirring continuously. Simmer for 1 minute, then remove from the heat and beat in the sugar and vanilla essence. Cover and leave to cool. Whip the cream until thick, fold through the custard and pour into an ice tray. Freeze until just firm.

Turn into a bowl and beat until smooth. Beat the egg white until stiff and fold through the mixture. Return to the ice tray and freeze until hard. Serve with wafers and raspberries, if available.

Brandy cornets

Brandy cornets

Metric	Imperial
25 g butter or margarine	1 oz butter or margarine
25 g golden syrup	1 oz golden syrup
40 g caster sugar	1½ oz caster sugar
25 g plain flour	1 oz plain flour
1 × 2.5 ml spoon ground ginger	½ teaspoon ground ginger
6 × 15 ml spoons double cream	6 tablespoons double cream
2–3 pieces stem ginger, chopped	2–3 pieces stem ginger, chopped

Cooking Time: About 30 minutes
Oven: 180°C, 350°F, Gas Mark 4

Put the butter or margarine, syrup and sugar into a saucepan and heat gently until the fat melts. Remove from the heat and beat in the flour and ground ginger. Place 5 ml spoons (teaspoons) of the mixture, well apart, on greased baking sheets. Bake towards the top of a preheated moderate oven for 8 to 10 minutes or until golden brown. Meanwhile, grease several wooden spoon handles or cream horn tins. Cool the biscuits for 1 to 2 minutes, then loosen with a palette knife and roll quickly around the handles or tins. Cool on wire racks until hard, then remove the handles or tins. Make the remaining biscuits in the same way.

Whip the cream until thick and fold in the chopped ginger. Spoon or pipe into the brandy cornets just before serving so they will remain crisp.

Blackberry and apple crisps

Metric	Imperial
100 g blackberries	4 oz blackberries
2 × 15 ml spoons water	2 tablespoons water
1–2 cooking apples, peeled, cored and sliced	1–2 cooking apples, peeled, cored and sliced
Sugar to taste	Sugar to taste
4 × 15 ml spoons double cream	4 tablespoons double cream
Topping:	Topping:
15 g butter	½ oz butter
1 × 15 ml spoon golden syrup	1 tablespoon golden syrup
20 g cornflakes	¾ oz cornflakes

Cooking Time: About 10 minutes

Stew the blackberries gently in the water for 5 minutes. Add the apples, cover and simmer gently until soft and pulpy. Sweeten to taste and leave to cool. Spoon into two glasses. Whip the cream until thick and spoon over the fruit.

Melt the butter in a saucepan. Stir in the syrup until well mixed, then add the cornflakes. Mix until thoroughly coated. Cool and spoon over the layer of cream.

Note: Other stewed fruits or jellied fruits can be served in this way.

Apple brulée

Metric

500 g cooking apples,
peeled, cored and sliced
2 × 15 ml spoons water
40–50 g sugar
150 ml double cream or
soured cream
1 × 5 ml spoon finely
grated orange or
grapefruit rind
Soft light brown sugar or
caster sugar

Imperial

1 lb cooking apples,
peeled, cored and sliced
2 tablespoons water
1½–2 oz sugar
¼ pint double cream or
soured cream
1 teaspoon finely grated
orange or grapefruit rind
Soft light brown sugar or
caster sugar

Cooking Time: About 10 minutes

Cook the apples in the water until soft, then continue to boil carefully, uncovered, until reduced to a thick purée. Sweeten to taste. Pour into a flameproof dish and leave to cool. Whip the double cream until thick (do not whip soured cream) and fold in the fruit rind. Spread over the apple and chill until just before required.

Cover the cream with a layer of sugar – about 1 cm (⅔ inch) thick. Put under a preheated hot grill and cook to melt the sugar. The dessert can be served while still bubbling or be left to cool and harden. The caramel will then need to be tapped sharply to break to serve.

Blackberry and apple crisps; Apple brulée

Hot fruit soufflé

Metric

1 small banana, sliced
1 × 200 g can apricot
halves, drained
25 g caster sugar
2 large eggs, separated
2 × 15 ml spoons plain
flour
150 ml milk
1 × 2.5 ml spoon vanilla
essence
Icing sugar

Imperial

1 small banana, sliced
1 × 7 oz can apricot
halves, drained
1 oz caster sugar
2 large eggs, separated
2 tablespoons plain flour
¼ pint milk
½ teaspoon vanilla essence
Icing sugar

Cooking Time: 35–40 minutes
Oven: 180°C, 350°F, Gas Mark 4

Lightly grease a 900 ml (1½ pint) soufflé dish. Cover the bottom with the banana slices, then with the apricots. Beat the sugar and one egg yolk together in a saucepan until creamy. Beat in the flour. Gradually beat in the milk and bring slowly to the boil, stirring continuously. Simmer for 2 minutes. Remove from the heat and cool slightly, then beat in the other egg yolk and the vanilla essence. Beat the egg whites until stiff and fold through the sauce. Spoon over the fruit. Bake in a preheated moderate oven for 35 to 40 minutes or until lightly browned, well risen and firm to the touch. Serve straight from the oven, sprinkled with icing sugar.

Note: The apricot syrup can be thickened with a little cornflour dissolved in cold water for a sauce.

Baked chocolate Alaska

Metric

½ chocolate Swiss roll
1 × 200 g can fruit (e.g.
raspberries, peaches,
pears), drained and syrup
reserved
1–2 × 15 ml spoons rum
(optional)
Small block of chocolate
ice cream (or half large
packet)
2 large egg whites
100 g caster sugar
Few strips of candied
angelica
4 glacé cherries, halved

Imperial

½ chocolate Swiss roll
1 × 7 oz can fruit (e.g.
raspberries, peaches,
pears), drained and syrup
reserved
1–2 tablespoons rum
(optional)
Small block of chocolate
ice cream (or half large
packet)
2 large egg whites
4 oz caster sugar
Few strips of candied
angelica
4 glacé cherries, halved

Cooking Time: About 3 minutes
Oven: 230°C, 450°F, Gas Mark 8

Slice the Swiss roll and arrange the slices in a circle on a flat ovenproof plate. Spoon over a little of the fruit syrup and/or the rum (if used), just to moisten the cake. Put the ice cream in the centre of the circle and pile the fruit on top. Beat the egg whites until stiff, then gradually beat in half the sugar, making sure the meringue is stiff again after each addition. Fold in the remaining sugar. Quickly spread the meringue all over the cake, fruit and ice cream so it is completely covered. Put immediately into a preheated very hot oven and cook for 2 to 3 minutes or until the meringue is lightly tinged brown. Decorate with candied angelica and glacé cherries and serve immediately.

Fried apple pancakes

Metric

Pancakes:
50 g plain flour
Pinch of salt
1 egg
150 ml milk
Lard for frying

Filling:
1 × 125 g can apple sauce
1.5 × 5 ml spoons ground
cinnamon
25 g sultanas
25 g butter or margarine
15 g caster sugar

Imperial

Pancakes:
2 oz plain flour
Pinch of salt
1 egg
¼ pint milk
Lard for frying

Filling:
1 × 4 oz can apple sauce
1½ teaspoons ground
cinnamon
1 oz sultanas
1 oz butter or margarine
½ oz caster sugar

Cooking Time: About 15 minutes

Sift the flour and salt into a bowl. Make a well in the centre and add the egg. Add the milk a little at a time and gradually beat to a smooth batter. Melt a little lard in a small 18 cm (7 inch) frying pan and add sufficient batter just to cover the bottom thinly. Cook for 1 to 2 minutes or until the underside is brown, then turn over and brown the other side. Transfer to a plate. Make 3 further pancakes in the same way.

Mix the apple sauce, 1 × 2.5 ml spoon (½ teaspoon) of the cinnamon and the sultanas together. Spread over the pancakes. Fold in the sides of each one and fold up to make a parcel. Fry the parcels gently in melted butter or margarine until browned on both sides. Serve hot, sprinkled with a mixture of the sugar and the remaining cinnamon, with cream.

Hot fruit soufflé; Baked chocolate Alaska; Fried apple pancakes

Fruited bread and butter pudding; Beignets with cherry sauce; Banana fritters; Almond stuffed peaches

Fruited bread and butter pudding

Metric

2–3 slices of bread (brown or white)
40 g butter
50 g raisins
25 g chopped mixed candied peel
1 × 2.5 ml spoon grated orange rind
2–3 × 15 ml spoons demerara sugar
1 large egg
250 ml milk
Little mixed spice or ground cinnamon
3–4 glacé cherries, halved (optional)

Imperial

2–3 slices of bread (brown or white)
1½ oz butter
2 oz raisins
1 oz chopped mixed candied peel
½ teaspoon grated orange rind
2–3 tablespoons demerara sugar
1 large egg
8 fl oz milk
Little mixed spice or ground cinnamon
3–4 glacé cherries, halved (optional)

Cooking Time: About 35–40 minutes
Oven: 180°C, 350°F, Gas Mark 4

Spread the bread with most of the butter. Use the remainder to grease a 600 ml (1 pint) ovenproof dish. Cut the bread into strips and arrange in layers, buttered side upwards, in the dish, sprinkling each layer with the raisins, peel, orange rind and most of the sugar. Beat the egg and milk together and strain into the dish. Leave to stand for 15 minutes. Sprinkle with spice and the remaining sugar and dot with glacé cherries, if used. Bake in a preheated moderate oven for 35–40 minutes or until set and lightly browned. Serve hot.

Note: Sultanas and/or currants can be used in place of raisins.

Beignets with cherry sauce

Metric

25 g butter or margarine
4 × 15 ml spoons water
35 g plain flour, sifted
Pinch of salt
1 large egg, beaten
Oil for deep frying
Little caster sugar mixed
with ground cinnamon

Cherry sauce:
25 g sugar
120 ml water
Finely pared rind of ½
lemon
1.5 × 5 ml spoons lemon
juice
Pinch of ground cinnamon
100 g fresh cherries,
halved and stoned, or
canned cherries (see
Note)
1.5 × 5 ml spoons
arrowroot dissolved in
1 × 15 ml spoon water

Imperial

1 oz butter or margarine
4 tablespoons water
1¼ oz plain flour, sifted
Pinch of salt
1 large egg, beaten
Oil for deep frying
Little caster sugar mixed
with ground cinnamon

Cherry sauce:
1 oz sugar
4 fl oz water
Finely pared rind of ½
lemon
1½ teaspoons lemon juice
Pinch of ground cinnamon
4 oz fresh cherries, halved
and stoned, or canned
cherries (see Note)
1½ teaspoons arrowroot
dissolved in 1 tablespoon
water

Cooking Time: About 15 minutes

Put the butter or margarine and water into a saucepan and heat until the fat melts. Bring to the boil. Remove from heat and beat in the flour and salt all at once. Continue beating until the mixture leaves the sides of the pan clean. Cool slightly, then gradually beat in the egg until smooth. To make the sauce dissolve the sugar in the water. Add the lemon rind, juice and cinnamon and boil for 2 to 3 minutes. Add the cherries and simmer for 5 to 6 minutes. Remove the rind and stir in the dissolved arrowroot. Simmer until thickened.

Heat the oil in a deep frying pan to 188°C, 370°F. Put the dough into a forcing bag fitted with a 2.5 cm (1 inch) nozzle and pipe into the fat, cutting at 2.5 cm (1 inch) intervals. Alternatively, drop in small spoonsful. As the beignets begin to brown and swell, turn over and cook until golden brown – about 5 minutes. Drain well, then toss in a mixture of sugar and cinnamon and serve with the sauce.

Note: If using canned red or black cherries, drain them well and use the syrup in place of water to make the sauce.

Banana fritters

Metric

40 g plain flour
Pinch of salt
1 × 5 ml spoon oil
3 × 15 ml spoons water
1 standard egg white
3 bananas
About 50 g butter, or oil
for deep frying
25–40 g caster sugar
Large pinch of ground
cinnamon or mixed spice

Imperial

1½ oz plain flour
Pinch of salt
1 teaspoon oil
3 tablespoons water
1 standard egg white
3 bananas
About 2 oz butter, or oil
for deep frying
1–1½ oz caster sugar
Large pinch of ground
cinnamon or mixed spice

Cooking Time: 4–5 minutes

Sift the flour and salt into a bowl and make a well in the centre. Add the oil and water and gradually work in the flour to make a smooth batter. Just before required, beat the egg white until stiff and fold through the batter.

Cut the bananas in half or into 2.5 cm (1 inch) pieces and coat evenly in the batter. Fry in melted butter or hot deep fat until golden brown (turning over if using butter). Drain on absorbent kitchen paper and serve hot, sprinkled with spiced sugar (spice mixed with the caster sugar).

Almond stuffed peaches

Metric

25 g butter
15 g icing sugar, sifted
40 g ground almonds
Few drops of almond
essence
1 × 2.5 ml spoon finely
grated orange rind
2 large fresh peaches,
peeled, halved and stoned
1 × 15 ml spoon brandy or
sherry
2 × 15 ml spoons orange
juice
25–50 g caster sugar

Imperial

1 oz butter
½ oz icing sugar, sifted
1½ oz ground almonds
Few drops of almond
essence
½ teaspoon finely grated
orange rind
2 large fresh peaches,
peeled, halved and stoned
1 tablespoon brandy or
sherry
2 tablespoons orange juice
1–2 oz caster sugar

Cooking Time: 35–40 minutes
Oven: 190°C, 375°F, Gas Mark 5

Cream half the butter with the icing sugar until soft, then beat in the ground almonds, almond essence and a little of the grated orange rind. Form into four equal balls. Press the filling balls into the cavities in the peach halves, then press the peach halves back together again. Place in a small ovenproof dish.

Melt the remaining butter and add the remaining orange rind, brandy or sherry and orange juice. Spoon over the peaches and sprinkle thickly with caster sugar. Bake in a preheated moderately hot oven for 25 to 30 minutes or until the sugar forms a syrupy glaze and the peaches are tender. Serve hot or cold with single cream.

Soufflé omelette

Soufflé omelette

Metric

3 large eggs, separated
3 × 15 ml spoons hot
water
15 g butter or margarine

Filling:
3 × 15 ml spoons
sweetened apple purée
50–75 g fresh or frozen
raspberries or strawberries
Icing sugar

Imperial

3 large eggs, separated
3 tablespoons hot water
½ oz butter or margarine

Filling:
3 tablespoons sweetened
apple purée
2–3 oz fresh or frozen
raspberries or strawberries
Icing sugar

Cooking Time: 8–10 minutes

Whisk the egg yolks with the water until pale yellow and fluffy. Beat the egg whites until stiff and fold evenly into the yolks. Melt the butter or margarine in a small frying pan and tip to coat it completely. Pour in the egg mixture and cook gently until fluffy and golden brown underneath. Put under a preheated fairly hot grill for a few minutes to set and lightly colour the surface.

Heat the apple purée gently and stir in the fruit. Spoon over the omelette. Loosen carefully, fold in half and slide onto a hot plate. Sprinkle with icing sugar and serve at once. (A hot jam sauce can be used instead.)

Baked apples Lucy

Crêpes suzette

Baked apples Lucy

Metric	Imperial
2 large cooking apples	2 large cooking apples
4 × 15 ml spoons demerara sugar	4 tablespoons demerara sugar
2 × 5 ml spoons rum, brandy or sherry	2 teaspoons rum, brandy or sherry
50–100 g raspberries, fresh, frozen or canned	2–4 oz raspberries, fresh, frozen or canned

Cooking Time: About 50 minutes
Oven: 180°C, 350°F, Gas Mark 4

Wash the apples and remove the cores using an apple corer. Score the skin all around the centre of the apples and stand each one on a square of foil. Fill the centres with sugar and pour on the rum, brandy or sherry. Draw the corners of the foil together at the top and twist tightly. Stand on a baking sheet and bake in a preheated moderate oven for 30 to 45 minutes or until tender but not too mushy. Unwrap the foil and fill the cavities with raspberries. Return to the oven, uncovered, and bake for 5 minutes. Serve hot with pouring cream.

Crêpes suzette

Metric	Imperial
50 g plain flour	2 oz plain flour
Pinch of salt	Pinch of salt
1 × 5 ml spoon caster sugar	1 teaspoon caster sugar
1 egg	1 egg
150 ml milk	¼ pint milk
About 25 g butter for frying	About 1 oz butter for frying
Orange slices to decorate	Orange slices to decorate
Sauce:	Sauce:
25 g caster sugar	1 oz caster sugar
25 g butter	1 oz butter
Grated rind of 1 small orange and ½ lemon	Grated rind of 1 small orange and ½ lemon
Juice of 1 orange	Juice of 1 orange
1 × 5 ml spoon lemon juice	1 teaspoon lemon juice
2–3 × 15 ml spoons orange-flavoured liqueur or brandy	2–3 tablespoons orange-flavoured liqueur or brandy

Cooking Time: About 15 minutes

Sift the flour, salt and sugar into a bowl. Make a well in the centre and add the egg. Add the milk a little at a time and gradually beat to a smooth batter. Melt a little butter in a small 18 cm (7 inch) frying pan and add sufficient batter just to cover the bottom very thinly. Cook for 1 to 2 minutes or until the underside is brown, then turn over and brown the other side. Transfer to a plate. Make 4 to 5 more very thin pancakes in the same way.

To make the sauce, put the sugar in a frying pan and heat gently until it melts and begins to brown. Add the butter, orange and lemon rinds and juices and heat until the caramel dissolves. Fold each pancake into four and add to the pan. Spoon the sauce over and heat through. Just before serving, warm the liqueur or brandy and pour into the pan. Set alight and serve, garnished with orange slices.